NEW DIRECTIONS FOR CHILD DEVELOPMENT

William Damon, *Brown University*
*EDITOR-IN-CHIEF*

# Children's Autonomy, Social Competence, and Interactions with Adults and Other Children: Exploring Connections and Consequences

Melanie Killen
*University of Maryland, College Park*

EDITOR

Number 73, Fall 1996

JOSSEY-BASS PUBLISHERS
San Francisco

CHILDREN'S AUTONOMY, SOCIAL COMPETENCE, AND INTERACTIONS WITH ADULTS
AND OTHER CHILDREN: EXPLORING CONNECTIONS AND CONSEQUENCES
*Melanie Killen* (ed.)
New Directions for Child Development, no. 73
*William Damon*, Editor-in-Chief

Microfilm copies of issues and articles are available in 16mm and 35mm,
as well as microfiche in 105mm, through University Microfilms Inc., 300
North Zeeb Road, Ann Arbor, Michigan 48106-1346.

ISSN 0195-2269        ISBN 0-7879-9894-X

NEW DIRECTIONS FOR CHILD DEVELOPMENT is part of The Jossey-Bass
Education Series and is published quarterly by Jossey-Bass Inc., Publishers,
350 Sansome Street, San Francisco, California 94104-1342. Periodicals
postage paid at San Francisco, California, and at additional mailing
offices. POSTMASTER: Send address changes to New Directions for Child
Development, Jossey-Bass Inc., Publishers, 350 Sansome Street, San Francisco, California 94104-1342.

SUBSCRIPTIONS cost $61.00 for individuals and $96.00 for institutions,
agencies, and libraries.

EDITORIAL CORRESPONDENCE should be sent to the Editor-in-Chief,
William Damon, Department of Education, Box 1938, Brown University,
Providence, Rhode Island 02912.

Cover photograph by Wernher Krutein/PHOTOVAULT © 1990.

TCF Manufactured in the United States of America on Lyons Falls
Pathfinder Tradebook. This paper is acid-free and 100 percent
totally chlorine-free.

# CONTENTS

# EDITOR'S NOTES

Autonomy is a recognized goal of development. The primary developmental work on autonomy has focused on self-concept (Damon and Hart, 1988), identity (Erikson, 1968), and personal agency (Nucci and Lee, 1993). Recently, researchers have extended this work by examining connections between children's autonomy and interpersonal development, including studying the ways in which the development of autonomy is connected to children's methods of conflict resolution (Killen and Nucci, 1995; Lewis, 1995; Chapter Five, this volume), social knowledge (Nucci and Lee, 1993), social competence with peers (Crockenberg and Litman, 1990), socioemotional knowledge (Chapter Two, this volume), and social coordination (Chapter Four, this volume). Traditionally, autonomy and social development have been located in disparate research literatures. The goal of this volume is to bring together the work of researchers who have investigated autonomy and social development and the links between the two.

Two themes have guided this endeavor: First, what are the means by which adults foster autonomy in children? And second, how does autonomy bear on the social and interpersonal aspects of development? The first issue concerns the role of adults. The studies described in this volume have revealed that adults foster autonomy through the use of *negotiation, reciprocity,* and *collaboration.* This pattern is in contrast to traditional characterizations of adult-child relationships. Traditional socialization theory characterized adult-child relationships in terms of a unidirectional transmission process from the adult, who acts as an agent of the society, to the child; traditional structural developmental theory characterized adult-child relationships in terms of unilateral respect (Piaget, 1932) and punishment (Kohlberg, 1984) (for reviews of these theoretical positions, see Grusec and Goodnow, 1994; Smetana, in press). What has contributed to this reformulation is an emphasis on identification of the context of the interaction and on the nature of the exchange.

The studies in this volume show that parents and teachers do not negotiate with children regarding all types of issues. Parents and teachers negotiate with children about events referred to as "personal" (those issues that children can legitimately decide, such as what to wear, what to eat, and who to play with)

Thanks are extended to Bill Damon for encouraging this issue of *New Directions for Child Development;* to the contributors for their timely and rich manuscripts; to graduate students at the University of Maryland George Bregman, Dora Chen, Stacey Horn, Karen L. Murphy, and Christine Theimer for engaging in useful discussions about autonomy and conflict resolution; to Bill Arsenio, Dan Hart, Larry Nucci, Hildy Ross, Judith Smetana, Elliot Turiel, and Cecilia Wainryb for collaborative projects on the topic; and to Paige Tinney-Reed for technical assistance.

(Chapter One, this volume). Moral conflicts, such as whether physical aggression should be used, are viewed as issues about which children should not make decisions (for example, it is not all right for a child to decide that hitting is OK). Yet particular types of adult intervention strategies, such as collaboration, enable children to work out social and moral conflicts on their own (for example, by assisting children to solve aggressive encounters with nonaggressive strategies) (Chapters Two, Three, Four, and Five, this volume). It is essential to recognize the differences between fostering autonomy for self-development (such as providing choice regarding what to wear) and fostering autonomy for social and moral development (for example, enabling children to work out conflicts on their own). This distinction is pervasive in this volume.

Thus the methods by which adults grant autonomy to children are both varied and complex. Variation is reflected in diverse cultural expectations, disparate parental styles, and multifaceted classroom approaches. Complexity occurs with respect to understanding the contextual constraints and domain specificity of the interaction. Decisions are made by adults regarding the nature of the issue, the history of interactions, and the parameters of the social setting.

The ways in which adults foster autonomy bear on the second theme of this volume: How does the fostering of autonomy relate to children's social and interpersonal development? When adults use explanations and rationales instead of simple commands, for example, children resolve conflicts with peers and siblings in constructive and nonaggressive ways (Bayer, Whaley, and May, 1995). A significant body of work has also shown that children who are granted autonomy are motivated to do well in the classroom (Deci and Ryan, 1985). Research has also shown that children who develop a positive sense of autonomy interact with peers in constructive ways, including by developing methods of negotiation and compromise, skills that are essential for conflict resolution strategies. As many of the contributors to this volume report, children's conflicts serve important social and developmental functions; through conflict, particularly with peers, children learn to negotiate, compromise, and bargain (see also Hay and Ross, 1982; Ross and Conant, 1992; Piaget, 1932; Shantz, 1987). Adults can play an important role in this aspect of development by assisting children to work out conflicts on their own (Chapters Four and Five, this volume). Investigating the means by which adults foster peer negotiation is central to the predominant goal of this volume, the relationship between autonomy and social development. Included is the work of researchers who have studied the multitude of ways in which fostering autonomy is connected to children's development of positive modes of social interaction and social competence.

The first chapter of this volume provides a model for examining the emergence of autonomy out of adult-child negotiation. Guided by social domain theory, Larry P. Nucci, Judith G. Smetana, and I describe several studies that have documented how adults negotiate with children about the personal (as noted earlier, those issues about which a child can make legitimate decisions). Their studies have shown that as children age they prefer that they rather than adults make decisions about personal issues. Their studies have also shown that parents and teachers differ in the ways they encourage autonomy. While they both provide children with choice regarding personal issues, and while they both use indirect messages about the personal, parents negotiate with children much more often than teachers do. Teachers' concerns with group order may make them less inclined to negotiate with children on an individual basis. Yet both parents and teachers recognize the domain of the personal and make attempts to grant children decision-making power in this type of interaction.

The second chapter describes the connections between autonomy and socioemotional development. William Arsenio and Sharon Cooperman find that children who respond to others in emotionally aversive ways during conflicts, and who overattribute positive emotions on the part of instigators, are less likely to use negotiation during conflicts and are potentially at risk of not developing social competence. Further, Arsenio and Cooperman show how teachers' methods of intervention differ for children of various sociometric statuses. Also, teachers intervene in disliked children's nonaggressive conflicts more often than in liked children's conflicts. One result of this pattern of intervention may be that disliked children are given fewer opportunities to develop the autonomy and social skills that are necessary for improving their peer relationships.

In the third chapter, Susan Crockenberg, Shelly Jackson, and Adela M. Langrock provide evidence to demonstrate that when parents collaborate with children, children's social competence with peers increases. Crockenberg and her colleagues have been at the forefront in contributing to the reconceptualization of the role of adults by showing how collaborative modes of interaction are very important for young children's social competence. The authors describe a study that suggests that children's social competence is more influenced by same-gender than by opposite-gender parents.

In the fourth chapter, Artin Göncü and Virginia Cannella present their model of social interaction, which analyzes the ways that teachers guide preschool-aged children through conflict resolution. Drawing on Piagetian and Vygotskyan theories to construct a framework for examining teacher-child discourse, Göncü and Cannella focus on the means by which culture has a direct influence on teacher resolution strategies. In their model, the adult and the child engage in a process called constructing intersubjectivity; the shared understanding among participants in an activity is accomplished through coordination of intentions. This is a clear departure from the traditional unidirectional characterization of adult-child relationships.

In the fifth chapter, Hildy Ross, Jacqueline Martin, Michal Perlman, Melissa Smith, Elizabeth Blackmore, and Jodie Hunter examine the predictions that different developmental models—Piagetian, socialization, and conflict mediation—make regarding the role of adults in children's conflicts. Ross and her associates apply these predictions to a series of studies they have conducted on sibling disputes in the home. They conclude that parental intervention techniques (nonintervention, authoritative intervention, or mediation) differ depending on the nature of the issue. Their observations reveal that parental interventions are largely focused on property damage and physical aggression, while on matters relating to ownership, parents are less authoritative; in fact, in such matters parents relinquish control and act as mediators in children's disputes. In general, however, parents use authoritative strategies, and children respond with tattling and appeals to adult intervention. One avenue for future research is whether children would use more negotiation if parents made more efforts to encourage autonomy and peer mediation. The authors also demonstrate the ways in which parents and children struggle to determine where the locus of decision lies in intrafamilial disputes.

The final chapter, by Catherine C. Lewis, addresses many of the issues discussed in the proceeding chapters by examining Japanese preschool education and philosophy. In her analysis of interactions in nineteen Japanese preschools, Lewis focuses on how Japanese preschool teachers diminish their role as authority figures with young children in order to encourage children to develop a sense of self-efficacy and autonomy. The most common Japanese adult response to conflicts is teacher-directed nonintervention ("Why don't you go tell Taro why you don't like being hit?"); adults rarely use commands and rule statements. One of the consequences of the Japanese strategy seems to be that Japanese children use a high level of negotiation in their interactions, with very little aggression. Lewis proposes that the use of compromise is a result of teachers' emphasizing belongingness and social competence in classroom interactions. By Lewis's account, an important aim of Japanese preschools is to coordinate both individual and group needs. This is in contrast to the traditional characterization of Japanese culture as collectivistic, in which the individual is subordinated to the group. Thus Lewis provides an interesting extension of the themes raised throughout the volume by describing how adults in a non-Western culture encourage autonomy and social competence among peers.

In sum, how adults foster autonomy varies by setting, type of issue, and cultural expectations; the connection between encouraging autonomy and constructive peer interaction is complex. Together these chapters provide an in-depth examination of the way in which autonomy is constructed out of social interaction with adults, and of the consequences this approach has for peer (and sibling) interaction and social competence. Each contributor to this volume provides a new window into understanding the links between social interactions and social developmental outcomes.

Melanie Killen
Editor

## References

Bayer, C. L., Whaley, K., and May, S. E. "Strategic Assistance in Toddler Disputes: II: Sequences and Patterns of Teachers' Message Strategies." *Early Education and Development*, 1995, 6, 405–432.

Crockenberg, S., and Litman, C. "Autonomy as Competence in Two-Year-Olds: Maternal Correlates of Child Defiance, Compliance, and Self-Assertion." *Developmental Psychology,* 1990, *26,* 961–971.

Damon, W., and Hart, D. *Self Understanding from Childhood to Adolescence.* New York: Cambridge University Press, 1988.

Deci, E. L., and Ryan, R. M. *Intrinsic Motivation and Self-Determination in Human Behavior.* New York: Plenum, 1985.

Erikson, E. *Identity: Youth and Crisis.* New York: Norton, 1968.

Grusec, J. E., and Goodnow, J. J. "Impact of Parental Discipline Methods on the Child's Internalization of Values: A Reconceptualization of Current Points of View." *Developmental Psychology,* 1994, *30,* 4–19.

Hay, D. F., and Ross, H. "The Social Nature of Early Conflict." *Child Development,* 1982, *53,* 105–113.

Killen, M., and Nucci, L. "Morality, Autonomy, and Social Conflict." In M. Killen and D. Hart (eds.), *Morality in Everyday Life: Developmental Perspectives.* New York: Cambridge University Press, 1995.

Kohlberg, L. *Essays on Moral Development.* Vol. 2: *The Psychology of Moral Development.* San Francisco: Harper San Francisco, 1984.

Lewis, C. C. *Educating Hearts and Minds: Reflections on Japanese Preschool and Elementary Education.* New York: Cambridge University Press, 1995.

Nucci, L. P., and Lee, J. Y. "Morality and Autonomy." In G. G. Noam and T. E. Wren (eds.), *The Moral Self.* Cambridge, Mass.: MIT Press, 1993.

Piaget, J. *The Moral Judgment of the Child.* New York: Free Press, 1932.

Ross, H. S., and Conant, C. L. "The Social Structure of Early Conflict: Interaction, Relationships, and Alliances." In C. U. Shantz and W. Hartup (eds.), *Conflict in Child and Adolescent Development.* New York: Cambridge University Press, 1992.

Shantz, C. U. "Conflicts Between Children." *Child Development,* 1987, *58,* 283–305.

Smetana, J. G. "Parenting and the Development of Social Knowledge Reconceptualized: A Social Domain Analysis." In J. E. Grusec and L. Kuczynski (eds.), *Handbook of Parenting and the Transmission of Values.* New York: Wiley, in press.

*MELANIE KILLEN is associate professor in the Department of Human Development and the Institute for Child Study at the University of Maryland, College Park.*

*This chapter asserts that the personal domain is constructed by children in their interactions with adults. It describes studies that document the ways in which children claim the personal domain and assert their autonomy.*

# Autonomy and the Personal: Negotiation and Social Reciprocity in Adult Child Social Exchanges

*Larry P. Nucci, Melanie Killen, Judith G. Smetana*

The emergence of children's autonomy involves two interrelated factors. One is the development of the child's competencies, and the other is the child's establishment of boundaries between what is within the child's area of privacy and personal discretion and what falls within the purview of normative regulation. With regard to the former, it is easy to see how newfound competencies, such as the ability to walk, provide the toddler with greater possibilities for autonomy than exist for the infant. Erikson (1963) was one of the first theorists to connect the emergence of competencies in early childhood with the child's assertion of personal authority over the self. The prevalence of children's noncompliance with parental authority within the "terrible twos," as Gesell (1928) referred to this period in development, was explained by Erikson as an expression of the child's efforts to establish bounded control over the self made salient by the child's emerging abilities to exert control over personal body functions (bladder and bowel control) and by the child's capacity to manipulate the environment through physical means (locomotion, manual dexterity) and by speech acts.

The key aspect of this period for Erikson was the child's negotiation of authority with the parent. According to Erikson, failure to establish a balance between the child's areas of discretion and the parent's representation

George Bregman, Dora Chen, Stacey Horn, Karen L. Murphy, and Christine Theimer provided invaluable assistance with data collection and data analysis for the study on autonomy in the preschool setting.

of societal regulation results in problems of psychological adjustment with far-reaching significance. Erikson's observations predated more recent depictions of the striving for control over a personal sphere of actions evident in early infancy (Mahler, 1979; Stern, 1985). They also preceded other work characterizing early- and middle-childhood noncompliance as evidence of a continuing exchange between children and adult authority over children's assertions of control over their own lives (Brehm and Brehm, 1981; Crockenberg and Litman, 1990; Stipek, Gralinski, and Kopp, 1990).

Running through all of this research and theory is a depiction of negotiation between children and adults as children strive to establish themselves as autonomous individuals. Yet what is being negotiated is left unspecified in these accounts of individuation and the development of children's autonomy. Our contribution to understanding the development of children's autonomy has been to provide a theoretical framework within which to address the specific nature of the child's claims to personal discretion as they relate to collective norms, authority, and interpersonal moral obligations, as well as to examine the social-interactional forms that the development of autonomy takes in early development. From within this framework we also address the relations between children's developing competencies and their broadening field of personal authority. Our approach is informed by what we refer to as social domain theory (Turiel, 1983). This view of social development holds that children construct social concepts within discrete conceptual and developmental systems that are generated out of qualitatively differing aspects of their social interactions (Turiel, 1983). These domains correspond to what Piaget ([1975] 1985) referred to as partial systems (or subsystems) with respect to the mind as a totality. Each partial system forms an internally equilibrated structure that in certain contexts may interact with other systems, requiring interdomain coordination. Conceptual domains, then, are understood to be dynamic systems of psychological equilibration (Piaget, [1975] 1985) and not static information-processing templates. Thus changes in one system have ramifications for the way issues are dealt with or understood within other conceptual systems.

Within domain theory, a distinction is drawn between children's understandings of moral and conventional regulation and their conceptions of the personal (Nucci, 1977, 1981, 1996). The personal is the set of actions that the individual considers to be outside the area of justifiable social regulation, subject not to considerations of right and wrong but to preferences and choice. This set of issues constitutes a circumscribed set of actions that define the bounds of individual authority. The child's identification of and maintenance of control over these issues is integral to the child's assertion of autonomy because it establishes the social border between the self and others. Functionally, exercise of choice within the personal permits the construction of what is socially unique about the person within the frame of socially ascribed roles and scripts (such as one's given name, gender, and social class). Structurally, concepts about the personal are formed by underlying conceptions of psychological entities of personhood and self (Nucci, 1977). The personal comprises the set of actions that permits the child to construct both a sense of the self as "object," or what James (1899) referred to as the "me," and the subjective sense of agency or authorship, or what James referred to as the "I." Examples of issues treated as personal by children and adolescents within North America include the content of one's correspondence and self-expressive creative works, one's recreational activities, one's choice of friends or intimates, and actions that focus on the state of one's own body (Nucci, 1981; Nucci, Guerra, and Lee, 1991; Killen, Leviton, and Cahill, 1991; Smetana, 1995a; Smetana, Bridgeman, and Turiel, 1983).

The child's construction of what is personal takes place within a larger social framework, and the establishment of an understanding of the personal is relative to the child's emerging understandings of convention (consensually established social norms) and morality (matters of fairness, welfare, and rights). Thus the content of the personal forms a circumscribed set of actions bounded not only by the child's understandings of what it means for something to be personal but also by the child's appreciation for morality and conventional regulation. In terms of development, the child's construction of what is private or personal is not an autochthonous achievement involving only the child's assertion of freedom of action. Rather, it is socially constructed out of negotiation and input from others (Nucci, 1996). Thus the precise content of what is personal will vary as a function of the general system of conventions within which the child operates and the degree to which the child has successfully established an area of personal authority. A considerable part of that variation is cultural in origin, and study of cultural variations in children's personal domains is an emerging area of interest (Killen and Nucci, 1995; Killen and Sueyoshi, 1995; Miller, Bersoff, and Harwood, 1990; Nucci, Camino, and Milnitsky-Sapiro, 1996; Yau and Smetana, 1996).

In addition to cultural and contextual variations in conventions, the relation between what children can claim to be personal and what they are permitted by adults to control is related to adult perceptions of children's competencies. As was noted earlier, a part of the interpersonal negotiation that results in children's autonomy is composed of a give-and-take between adults and children over the child's capacity to carry out activity in ways that do not pose undue risks to the child's health and safety. Understanding these issues of personal well-being constitutes an additional conceptual frame from which the child evaluates her personal authority in relation to objective, nonsocial prudential considerations (Tisak and Turiel, 1984). With age, as the child's competencies increase, control over prudential issues shifts from the parent to the child, as a function of both the parent's release of control and the child's assertion of personal authority over the self (Smetana, 1988a, 1988b).

In our studies of adult-child interactions and children's autonomy, we have analyzed how adults provide choice to children and how children assert their choices regarding personal issues. The provision of choice and privacy needs to be differentiated from related adult efforts to foster children's competencies by allowing them to work out their own solutions to social or practical problems.

In the latter cases, adults are engaging in a form of pedagogy based on an intuitive understanding of the nature of child development and the limitations of direct instruction. In effect, adults allow the natural feedback resulting from the child's actions to serve as the child's teacher. Perhaps the most prosaic universal example would be that of the parent who stands aside while a one-year-old child attempts repeatedly to stand up and walk on his or her own. Piaget (1932) argued that in the social arena children's moral competence was enhanced by adults who diminished their power relative to children and allowed them opportunities to construct solutions to moral disputes among themselves. Likewise, the constructivist educator Constance Kamii (1984) advocates classroom practices that engage children in collaborative efforts at problem solving as a way of fostering children's logical-mathematical understandings. In each of these cases, what is expected to develop are sets of competencies that result in nonarbitrary and compelling outcomes (such as conceptions of number conservation, and moral reciprocity). In other cases, as when a parent stands aside to allow a child to work through the personal disappointment resulting from a decision to spend allowance money on a flashy but poorly constructed toy, issues of personal choice and the fostering of competence (thoughtful shopping) converge. In each of these situations, opportunities are provided for children to experience their own sense of agency and their capacity to operate independently from adult guidance. This sense of agency is fundamental to a sense of self (James, 1899). The development of social competencies in and of themselves, however, is not sufficient for the child to construct a sense of self as unique and individual. Autonomy characterized by a sense of individuality emerges out of the child's freedom of action within the personal domain (Nucci, 1996).

In general, then, opportunities to make decisions allow the child a sense of self-efficacy. Yet in some types of situations, such as when one child bullies another child or creates a social disturbance in a group situation, the costs of parents' granting choice are outweighed by the benefits of asserting control. In these situations, adults refrain from granting autonomy in order to uphold and preserve the moral or societal order. Therefore we hypothesize that adults do not grant decision-making authority for all types of issues in the same way. We would expect that adults typically assert more control and use more directives when dealing with moral, social-conventional, and prudential issues than when responding to children's assertions regarding personal (nonprudential) events. This is because children can legitimately decide what to do about issues in the personal domain; there are no negative consequences to others (as with moral transgressions) or to the social order (as with conventional violations). By definition, personal issues (such as what to wear or what name to use) are those that affect the self and not others. With regard to prudential issues, we would expect parents to exert control to the extent that they view their children as unable to make wise decisions regarding their personal welfare. With young children, in particular, we would expect parents to exert control in most cases entailing matters of the children's health or safety.

Research on children's autonomy is not extensive. Few studies have focused on the types of choices children are granted or the domains in which autonomy is asserted. Instead, research typically has focused on parental behaviors and has investigated relationships between maternal control strategies and children's defiant and compliant behavior. For instance, in their summary of the literature, Crockenberg and Litman (1990) reported that children who use verbal refusals ("no") have been shown to demonstrate more negotiation with their mothers (Kuczynski, Kochanska, Radke-Yarrow, and Girnius-Brown, 1987), to be more developmentally advanced (Vaughn, Kopp, and Krakow, 1984), and to be more likely to be securely attached (Matas, Arend, and Sroufe, 1978) than children who demonstrate defiance. Crockenberg and Litman further distinguished between child defiance, compliance, and self-assertion regarding mother-child interactions during a clean-up-toys task. In their study, they found that mothers' use of power assertion (in the form of negative control) was highly related to children's defiance, and that mothers' use of control and guidance produced more positive forms of child autonomy such as self-assertion. Thus Crockenberg and Litman (1990) demonstrated that in early childhood, autonomy expressed as self-assertion is more socially competent than autonomy expressed as defiance. The importance of this research is that it has provided distinctions regarding early expressions of autonomy.

In our analyses, we have been examining in some detail the different ways that children and adults negotiate autonomy and how children assert (and adults grant) autonomy regarding events that are within the child's personal domain (Nucci and Weber, 1995; Killen and Smetana, 1996). Events identified within the personal domain of young children have included what to wear, what to eat, what to play, and choice of playmates in both home and school settings. The focus in the current chapter is on our work with young children. In related work, we have examined the ways in which parents and adolescents negotiate the gradual assumption of prudential issues as subject to adolescent rather than parental control (Tisak and Tisak, 1990; Smetana, 1995a).

In sum, social domain theory views the development of children's autonomy as a multifaceted interplay among children's developing competencies and their conceptions of morality, convention, and the personal. Personal autonomy coexists with moral and societal constraints as components of qualitatively differing aspects of social existence, rather than as polar opposites on a continuum. By understanding the relationship in this way, we can begin to explore the emergence of autonomy within the concurrent development of the child's sense of interpersonal and social responsibility.

## Studies of Social Interaction and the Personal Domain in Young Children

We turn now to a discussion of recent studies on the emergence of personal autonomy in young children. Three research projects are described: one on mother-child interactions in the home, the second a follow-up interview study of mothers' conceptions of children's areas of personal autonomy, and the third a study on teacher-child interactions in preschool classrooms. In each study, our focus was on children who were beyond two years of age. This allowed us to look at the development of autonomy in children older than the "terrible twos" or beyond the "autonomy versus shame and doubt" period (Erikson, 1963) about which so much has already been written. In addition, studying preschool-aged children afforded us the opportunity to conduct interviews regarding the children's own conceptions of various social rules and acts.

The two contexts for the studies, home and school, comprise the main areas of adult-child contact for young children. In addition, they represent different layers of conventional regulation within which children must assert their areas of personal discretion and autonomy. Exploring these contexts allows us to examine the negotiation processes that take place between children and adults as children construct a sense of themselves as autonomous individuals within differing social institutional settings. These settings vary not only in terms of degree and type of social regulation but also in terms of the nature of the interpersonal relationships that exist. On the basis of an interview study conducted with somewhat older children (Weber, 1996), we know that within the first year of formal schooling children are aware that home and school are different normative environments. Moreover, during first grade, children perceive school to be a more constraining environment than home, and one in which opportunities for negotiation are limited and in which children almost never prevail in a dispute with adult authority (Weber, 1996). Nonetheless, first graders perceive themselves as legitimately entitled to areas of choice and privacy at school as well as at home. These nascent understandings of personal autonomy are differentiated from the children's developing conceptualizations of the social, organizational, and protective functions of conventional and moral regulation within both contexts (Weber, 1996). In the studies described in this chapter, observations were made in both the home and preschool contexts of naturally occurring events related to issues of normative regulation and children's personal choice. In addition, interviews were conducted with both children and adults.

**The Emergence of the Personal in At-Home Mother-Child Interactions.** As a first step in examining the pattern of mother-child interactions associated with personal issues, Nucci and Weber (1995) conducted an observational study with twenty middle-class suburban mothers and their three- or four-year-old children. This particular sample was chosen on the assumption that members of the middle-class, because of their presumed cultural valuation of rights and individual freedom (Miller, Bersoff, and Harwood, 1990; Shweder, Mahapatra, and Miller, 1987), would be likely to engage in social exchanges pertaining to their children's personal domain. In the study, mother-child dyads were observed over a span of three days during four activity periods: early morning, when the child awoke, dressed, and had breakfast; daytime free play with a second child (sibling or friend) present; late afternoon and evening, including dinner; and bedtime, which included giving the child a bath. Trained coders classified transcribed event sequences as moral, conventional, prudential, personal, or mixed.

These interaction sequences were then examined in several ways. First, the overall form of the interactions was classified as to whether the social messages directed at children contained explicit or indirect information about the social meaning of a given action. Statements such as "that hurts" or "you are not allowed to swear" or "that's your business" were classified as direct. Statements such as "what do you say?" which served as reminders of expected behavior, or "would you like some more milk?" which offered choices, were coded as indirect. Second, a global assessment was made of whether the interaction resulted in negotiation involving some degree of concession by the mother. Finally, mothers' and children's individual statements and actions were assigned to specific behavioral categories.

As was expected, mother-child interactions were observed to take place over children's personal issues. The distribution of these personal events was as follows: food type/amount, 37 percent; activities (form of play, and so on), 31 percent; dress, 15 percent; body status (hairstyle, cleanliness), 7 percent; and playmate selection, 3 percent. Analyses of the overall form of interactions indicated that mothers tended to give direct descriptive social messages to children about moral and conventional acts as well as about actions involving prudence. In contrast, mothers' responses to personal events often entailed indirect or tacit social messages. Mothers rarely labeled personal matters as such. Instead, mothers differentially addressed the personal through the use of choices offered to the child, and to a lesser extent through the use of direct prerogative statements (such as "that's up to you" or "it's your own business"). Thus, with respect to the personal, it was largely left to the child to attach a social meaning to such issues. Interestingly, the content of observed interactions involving choices offered to children corresponded to the content of actions that mothers listed in a subsequent interview study as ones that ought to be up to children to control (Nucci and Smetana, 1996). There was a greater tendency for mothers to use direct messages in the context of moral, conventional, and prudential events than in the context of personal ones. This in itself is an indication that mothers view the former as issues in which the child needs to accommodate to specific external social demands and meanings, while the personal issues are for the child to idiosyncratically interpret and control. This differential overall response pattern was also evident in mothers' tendencies to negotiate in response to children's resistances to the mothers' behavioral requests for a given social action.

Mothers almost never negotiated with children regarding moral, conventional, or prudential forms of conduct. Conversely, nearly one-quarter of the observed interactions around personal issues involved negotiation and concession on the part of the mothers. What is also interesting is the degree to which negotiations took place in the context of mixed events. Over 90 percent of the observed mixed events involved overlap with the personal domain. Mothers engaged in negotiation with their children in the context of such mixed events about half of the time. This type of interaction over a mixed issue is illustrated in the following dialogue:

MOTHER:  Evan, it's your last day of nursery school. Why don't you wear your nursery sweatshirt?

CHILD:  I don't want to wear that one.

MOTHER:  This is the last day of nursery school, that's why we wear it. You want to wear that one?

CHILD:  Another one.

MOTHER:  Are you going to get it, or should I?

CHILD:  I will. First I got to get a shirt.

MOTHER:  [*Goes to the child's dresser and starts picking out shirts*]  This one? This one? Do you know which one you have in mind? Here, this is a new one.

CHILD:  No, it's too big.

MOTHER:  Oh, Evan, just wear it, and when you get home you can pick whatever you want, and I won't even help you. [*Child puts on shirt.*]

This case presents a conflict between a dress convention (wearing a particular sweatshirt on the last day of school) and the child's view that what to wear is a personal choice. The mother acknowledges the child's position and attempts to negotiate, finally offering the child a free choice once school is over. This example illustrates several things. For one, the mother provided direct information to the child about the convention in question: "This is the last day of nursery school, that's why we wear it." At the same time, the mother exhibited an interest in fostering the child's autonomy and decision making around the issue. The child's resistance, which conveyed the child's personal interest, was not simply cut off but was guided by the mother, who linked it to the child's autonomy: "Are you going to get it, or should I?" "You can pick whatever you want, and I won't even help you." In the end, there is compromise. The child got to choose, but within a more general conventional demand (enforced by the mother) that he wear a particular shirt.

The above exchange illustrates that the mothers in this study acted in ways that were concordant with an understanding that children should have areas of discretion and personal control. The excerpt also illustrates ways in which children, through their resistances, provided mothers with information about the children's desires and needs for personal choice. It is important to point out in this regard that children in the study did not exhibit a general or overall tendency to resist parental authority. Analyses of the individual responses provided by children indicated that assertions of prerogative and personal choice did not occur to the same degree across all forms of social interaction but were disproportionately associated with events involving personal issues. Assertions of prerogative and choice made up 88 percent of children's responses in the context of mixed events and 98 percent of their responses in the case of predominantly personal events. In contrast, such responses made up less than 10 percent of children's statements in the context of moral or prudential events and about 20 percent of their responses to conventional events.

The picture that emerges from these observations is of a differentiated pattern of social interactions in which the give-and-take between mothers and children is a function of the domain of the issue at hand. The child's construction of personal autonomy takes place within this differentiated and multifaceted set of social contexts. Mothers and children, at least by the child's third birthday, are not engaged in a random pattern of child resistance and adult control as would be suggested by a behaviorist account of socialization. There was no evidence of a process of shaping and curtailing children's random patterns of misbehavior. Nor were children reported to have engaged in across-the-board acts of defiance or noncompliance as would be suggested in global stage descriptions of the emergence of autonomy in early childhood (Erikson, 1963) or in characterizations of young children as engaged in a generalized resistance to adult authority (Brehm and Brehm, 1981; Kuczynski, Kochanska, Radke-Yarrow, and Girnius-Brown, 1987). Instead, it would appear that the child's efforts to assert freedom of action are domain dependent and generally limited to issues that touch on the child's personal domain. For their part, mothers provide opportunities for choice and prerogative, often offering such choices spontaneously without the child's instigation. In cases of conflict, mothers remain firm with respect to matters of convention, morality, and prudence, and enter into negotiation with children over issues pertinent to the child's personal area. These incidents of negotiation are themselves evidence that what is being worked out between mother and child are the boundaries between what is personal and what is expected of children participating within a particular family system.

The behavioral evidence obtained by Nucci and Weber (1995) would suggest that middle-class preschool-aged children differentiate the personal from matters of interpersonal social regulation. Interviews conducted with the children at the completion of the observations supported that interpretation. In response to questions regarding who should be the one to decide a given issue, the child or the mother, children indicated that they viewed personal but not moral or conventional behaviors as ones that should be up to the "self" and not for the mother to decide. The interviews also revealed, however, that at these young ages children have unstable conceptions of the degree to which they should have control over such issues. When children were asked whether it would be all right for the mother to tell the child what to do and whether the child should do what the mother says, children, as expected, were highly likely to state that the child should comply with the adult, and that the adult had legitimate authority with respect to moral or conventional issues. Conversely, the tendency for these young children to take the position that the child should not comply with the adult or that the adult did not have authority with regard to personal issues did not reach statistical significance. Thus, consistent with other reports (Tisak and Tisak, 1990), young children's sense of what is really up to them rather than their parents is not cut-and-dried but appears instead to be emergent.

**Mothers' Beliefs About the Personal Domain of Children.** In a follow-up to the Nucci and Weber (1995) investigation of mother-child interactions, an interview study was conducted within the same community and a neighboring suburb to obtain mothers' views on the issue of the personal domain of children (Nucci and Smetana, 1996). The study examined the beliefs of forty mothers with children either four or six years of age. Subjects in the study ranged from working- to upper-middle-class, with annual family incomes from $20,000 to in excess of $100,000. Parental education levels ranged from not having finished high school to having earned advanced professional degrees or doctorates. The interview comprised a set of open-ended questions that focused on the mothers' conceptions of whether children should be given decision-making authority and around what sorts of issues, and around which issues mothers should exert their authority. They were asked to explain on what bases they determined which behaviors to leave up to their children, and why they allowed or encouraged children to determine those things for themselves. Mothers were also queried about their sense of what issues generated conflicts between themselves and their children, how these conflicts were resolved, and what role they saw themselves playing in those mother-child exchanges. At the completion of the open-ended interview, mothers were given a sorting task in which they were presented with sets of hypothetical scenarios depicting children engaged in actions that exemplified transgressions of moral or conventional norms or prudential (safety) concerns, along with scenarios depicting children engaged in actions that fit the definition of the personal domain, and scenarios that were multifaceted or mixed, in which prudential or conventional concerns overlapped with personal ones. For each scenario, mothers were asked to indicate whether the act was one the mother should control, whether it was up to the child, or whether it was negotiable and could go either way.

All of the mothers interviewed in this study supported the notion that children four to seven years of age should be allowed choice over some things and that children should be allowed to hold their own opinions. Mothers justified allowing children to exercise choice on the grounds that decision making fostered competence and that allowing children to hold opinions of their own fostered the development of the child's agency and self-esteem. Thus these mothers appeared to value permitting their children areas of freedom in order to foster their personal development and autonomy. Consistent with the findings observed in the sorting task, however, mothers placed boundaries around actions they left up to children to determine. Mothers stated that their children were allowed to exercise choice over such personal issues as play activities, playmates, amount and type of food, and choice of clothes. Conversely, mothers stated that they placed limits on children's actions when those actions were counter to family or societal conventions and when they posed risks to the child or others. The mothers' responses to issues mentioned in this study were in line with the ways in which mothers responded to three- and four-year-old children in naturally occurring at-home interactions as observed by Nucci and Weber (1995).

Mothers stated that in addition to limiting children's activities when they conflicted with conventional, moral, or prudential considerations, they occasionally limited their children's activities in the very areas they had stated they allowed children to determine or control. As Nucci and Weber (1995) observed, mother-child conflicts over these personal issues often resulted in compromise by the adult. In the interviews conducted by Nucci and Smetana (1996), mothers expressed a willingness to compromise over such issues in order to support the child's agency, self-esteem, and competence. Mothers viewed themselves as acting rationally and pragmatically in response to their perceptions of the child's personal competence and the risks a given act posed to the child. In the context of mother-child disagreements, mothers tended to see themselves primarily as educators, and less often as controllers or nurturers.

When placed in the context of the results of at-home observations (Nucci and Weber, 1995), these interviews with mothers provide an integrated portrait of how mothers and preschool-aged children across the broad range of the North American middle-class establish and foster the emergence of the child's autonomy and sense of a personal domain of privacy and choice. The picture that emerges is not one of across-the-board struggle and conflict but rather of a shared and differentiated worldview in which autonomy and choice are coextant with obedience and conformity to common norms and rational moral and prudential constraints. Those conflicts that do arise are not random but generally fall within the range of issues at the edge of the child's competence to act in ways that are prudent (as viewed by the parent), or they are at the intersection of the norms of the social order and the child's arena of personal discretion.

**Autonomy and Children's Evaluations of the Personal in the Preschool Classroom.** The work thus far described focused on young children's interactions in the family. We turn now to a recent study (Killen and Smetana, 1996) that explored adult-child social interactions regarding personal issues within the more constrained, rule-bound setting of the preschool classroom. Prior research (Smetana and Bitz, 1996) had indicated that adolescents recognize that certain issues are within the realm of personal jurisdiction in school settings (such as choice of hairstyle and whom to sit next to in class) and that other issues may be treated as personal in other contexts but are legitimately constrained and regulated in school (such as when one expresses affection to boyfriends or girlfriends or leaves the classroom to go to the lavatory). Research on first graders has indicated that even young children understand that there are contextual differences in the boundaries of personal control (Weber, 1996). With that work as a backdrop, Killen and Smetana conducted observations of naturally occurring classroom interactions between preschool children and teachers, with the expectation that the patterns of adult-child interchanges in the preschool would, as in the home context, include interactions regarding issues of children's areas of personal choice and discretion. This study also explored, through interviews, whether young children maintain differentiated concepts of personal issues in the preschool classroom context.

Twenty preschool classrooms, half containing three-year-olds and half containing four-year-olds, were observed. Consistent with the studies just described, the preschools primarily served white middle-class children. Teacher-child interactions regarding personal control events were observed during three contexts: circle time, activity time, and lunch time. Personal control events were defined as those in which children could legitimately decide what to do without negative consequences for others. Thus, during circle time, personal control events included exchanges regarding where and how to sit; during activity time, personal control events included what activity to choose; and during lunch time, personal issues included what and how to eat and where to sit.

An analysis of 1,484 events (857 personal control events and 627 moral and social-conventional conflicts) revealed that like mothers in the home (Nucci and Weber, 1995), teachers tended to provide indirect messages, such as hints, choices, and questions, for personal events. In contrast, they used more direct messages, such as commands and rule statements, for moral and social-conventional events. Unlike mothers in the home, however, teachers did not negotiate personal events with children. In this respect, interactions with teachers regarding events in the personal domain resembled interactions regarding moral and social-conventional conflicts, which also were not negotiated. This observation is consistent with the self-reports of first graders (Weber, 1996), who claimed that teachers rarely negotiated and never allowed a child to win a dispute in the school context regarding an issue the child regarded as a personal matter but the teacher viewed as within the teacher's area of control.

To reiterate, the provision of personal choice in the classroom emerged both from statements by teachers asking children to express a preference or offering them choice and from children's own proactive assertions of preference or choice. In cases where teachers provided choices, children almost always responded positively to those opportunities. In cases where children proactively asserted choices, teachers simply either affirmed or negated the children's choices. Thus, although young children are provided occasions to construct a sense of personal choice and prerogative within the school context, their opportunities are more constrained than at home. The most marked difference would appear to be the lack of opportunities for adult-child negotiation within the classroom. The observed patterns did not vary by child age. Classrooms with three-year-olds did not differ from classrooms serving four-year-olds in teacher-child exchanges regarding personal control events.

**Children's Concepts About Personal Issues in the Preschool.** Many of the three- and four-year-olds from these classrooms, as well as an additional group of five-year-olds from the same preschools, were also interviewed to examine their conceptions of personal issues and decision making in the classroom. Equal numbers of primarily white middle-class boys and girls three, four, and five years of age ($n = 120$) were interviewed about four issues: where to sit at group time, what to eat at lunch, what to wear, and what activity to choose at activity time. These issues were drawn from the observations and

represented decisions a child can legitimately make without negative consequences to others' welfare or rights (moral transgressions), the social group
(conventional transgressions), or the self (prudential issues such as self-harm).
Each issue was presented as a scenario in which a child's choice conflicted with
a teacher's directive—for example, in the activity time scenario, a child wanted
to draw pictures and the teacher instructed the child to play with blocks. Children were interviewed about different dimensions of decision making related
to the personal, such as whether the child should comply with the teacher's
request, whether it is legitimate for the teacher to ask the child to engage in an
act, and who should make decisions about these acts (the child or the teacher).

The results were consistent across all questions and demonstrated age-
related shifts in children's judgments about the personal domain. Whereas
fewer than half (45 percent) of the three- and four-year-olds judged that children, not teachers, should make decisions about personal issues, the majority
(65 percent) of five-year-olds viewed these decisions as legitimately up to the
child rather than teachers. These age-related shifts in the tendency to view
issues as personal were concordant with age-related shifts in the types of justifications children provided for identifying acts as personal matters. The
majority of the five-year-olds reasoned about personal issues using personal
justifications, but this was not the case for the three- and four-year-olds, who
primarily gave undifferentiated reasons (such as, "Jenny should decide." Why?
"Because she should."). Five-year-olds' justifications were quite explicit about
the child's preference, desires, wants, and prerogatives, as the following example of an interview with a five-year-old girl illustrates:

INTERVIEWER: [Teacher wants Jenny to wear her red sweater, and Jenny wants to
wear the yellow one] Should Jenny wear the red sweater?
CHILD: She should wear the yellow sweater because she knows what to wear
and what is right.
INTERVIEWER: Who should decide what Jenny should wear outside, Jenny or
the teacher?
CHILD: Jenny, because Jenny is the boss of herself.
INTERVIEWER: If the teacher didn't tell Jenny to wear her red one, would it be
all right for her to wear the one that she wants to?
CHILD: Yes, because she's the boss of her own self.

This child viewed wearing a sweater as a decision legitimately within the
child's authority. Similar statements were obtained from other children in
response to other stories. For instance, in the scenario about what to eat at
lunch, a five-year-old boy stated, "Jimmy should decide what to eat." Why?
"Because he is the master of his lunch." Another child stated, "Susie should
decide what activity she does." Why? "Because she's her own self; she should
do what she wants."

The results of these interviews indicate that three-, four-, and five-year-old
children are beginning to construct a sense of personal discretion regarding

actions within the school context. It is interesting to note, however, that the percentages of preschool-aged children reported by Killen and Smetana (1996) as claiming jurisdiction over personal actions in school contexts was considerably lower than that reported by Nucci and Weber (1995) for children of the same age regarding events in the home context. Whether these context-related differences in the results from these two studies reflect reliable context-related differences in children's judgments needs to be pursued further. The finding of home-school differences in children's tendencies to view issues as personal is consistent, however, with results from Weber's (1996) interviews with first graders in which children explicitly acknowledged that school is less individualized and more focused on institutional collective learning goals than is the family context.

Taken together, the results of the classroom observations and preschool interviews of the Killen and Smetana (1996) study present a complex picture of the emergence of autonomy and children's conceptions of a personal domain in the classroom. On the one hand, teachers encourage children's autonomy in preschool by providing choice regarding activities, food, and participation in circle time. On the other hand, teachers rarely negotiate with children regarding the personal in ways that Nucci and Weber (1995) observed in primarily white middle-class North American homes. Therefore, although teachers may view the facilitation of autonomy development as an important goal of the preschool classroom, it is likely that this goal is subordinated to other goals, such as maintaining order and fostering group activities. The more constrained nature of personal control in the classroom relative to the home was reflected in the results of the interview portion of the Killen and Smetana study. Preschool children did not evidence a firm sense of personal prerogatives in the preschool setting until age five, when the majority of children evaluated some issues as legitimately up to the child to decide, based on concerns with agency and individuality. The later emergence of children's personal reasoning and judgments in the classroom as compared to the home (as described by Nucci and Weber, 1995) suggests that children's construction of stable conceptions of the personal entails progressive coordination of personal claims with the different and sometimes conflicting mixture of goals and organizational structures presented by contrasting social contexts (Weber, 1996).

## Extensions of the Personal with Age

The results of the three studies described here point to the emergence during early childhood of children's understanding of personal issues and the social interactions that facilitate social development. It should be clear from the foregoing discussion, however, that although an understanding of personal issues arises during the preschool years, the boundary between the child's developing autonomy and conventional regulation is continually negotiated both within and across contexts (for instance, between home and school) and across developmental periods. Children's understanding of personal issues is emergent during the preschool years and continues to develop. As children's competencies increase, we would expect a corresponding increase in their claims to personal control. This assertion has been supported in a series of studies examining children's claims to personal jurisdiction in the transition to and during adolescence (Smetana, 1988a, 1988b, 1995b; Smetana and Asquith, 1994). These studies have examined children's and parents' judgments of legitimate parental authority and adolescents' personal jurisdiction regarding hypothetical moral, conventional, prudential, and personal issues.

Several consistent findings have emerged from these studies. Among primarily white middle-class families, both adolescents and their parents have been found to view moral and conventional issues as legitimately regulated by parents, with little disagreement between parents and adolescents in these judgments. Among these same families, both adolescents and their parents also view a set of issues—such as what clothes to wear, choice of hairstyles, choice of friends, and how to spend allowance money—as personal and legitimately regulated by adolescents. However, what is seen as within the adolescents' arena of personal discretion increases dramatically from preadolescence to late adolescence, with parents consistently lagging behind adolescents in their willingness to grant their children autonomy over these issues. Moreover, related studies of adolescents' and parents' reasoning about parent-child conflict among both middle-class primarily white North American families (Smetana, 1988b, 1989; Smetana and Asquith, 1994) and lower-class Chinese adolescents in Hong Kong (Yau and Smetana, 1996) indicate that conflict occurs over where the boundaries between adolescents' personal jurisdiction and parents' legitimate authority should be drawn. Thus adolescent-parent conflict appears to provide a context in which the boundaries of adolescents' autonomy are renegotiated. This research underscores the importance of negotiation in the development of autonomy and also illustrates the active role of adolescents in claiming autonomy from their parents.

## Conclusion

Each family and school is embedded within the larger cultural and societal complex of norms and expectations. As children sort out the extensive properties of the class of actions within their personal domain across various contexts and within a variety of institutional settings, they establish autonomous and unique personal identities within a cultural frame (Nucci, 1996). This process reflects both a set of underlying features of psychological reality (the need to establish and maintain personal agency and a unique identity) and the inherent situatedness of any individual life. It is also linked to development as children move progressively toward adulthood and connect their areas of discretion to their emerging intellectual and social competence (Smetana, 1988a, 1988b, 1995b; Smetana and Asquith, 1994).

The studies we have focused on in this chapter were conducted within a sociocultural context that construes these issues in a particular way. In related work, we have begun to examine the ways in which the interplay between the personal and areas of interpersonal or social regulation is sorted out by individuals within a variety of cultural settings (Nucci, Camino, and Milnitsky-Sapiro, 1996; Yau and Smetana, 1996; Wainryb and Turiel, 1994). In that work, we have looked at the ways that class and culture may constrain or enlarge the areas of personal autonomy and rights. What we have been finding is that the emergence of personal autonomy is not confined to so-called individualistic cultures. Moreover, the general developmental pattern of progressive extension and consolidation of a personal domain as children age, particularly in adolescence, appears to be a cross-cultural rather than a Western phenomenon (Nucci, Camino, and Milnitsky-Sapiro, 1996; Yau and Smetana, 1996). At the same time, these cross-cultural studies have revealed considerable differences in the ways in which autonomy and its attendant rights are experienced and distributed as a function of gender, class, and cultural factors (Turiel, 1996). Thus there is a need for additional research to look at the ways in which culture interfaces with the construction of personal autonomy. It is our view that cross-cultural work that examines these issues from the theoretical framework outlined in this chapter will permit an analysis that moves beyond the overly simple heuristic of dividing up cultures into those categorized as individualistic and those categorized as collectivistic (Triandis, 1990). If, as we would claim, the construction of personal autonomy is a human developmental phenomenon, then the purpose of such future cross-cultural work will be to capture and accurately describe not only the particulars of development within a given cultural frame but also the nature and processes of human development that generalize across culture and context.

## References

Brehm, S. S., and Brehm, J. W. *Psychological Reaction: A Theory of Freedom and Control.* Orlando, Fla.: Academic Press, 1981.

Crockenberg, S., and Litman, C. "Autonomy as Competence in Two-Year-Olds: Maternal Correlates of Child Defiance, Compliance, and Self-Assertion." *Developmental Psychology,* 1990, *26,* 961–971.

Erikson, E. *Childhood and Society.* New York: Norton, 1963.

Gesell, A. *Infancy and Human Growth.* Old Tappan, N.J.: Macmillan, 1928.

James, W. *The Principles of Psychology.* London: Macmillan, 1899.

Kamii, C. "Autonomy: The Aim of Education Envisioned by Piaget." *Phi Delta Kappan,* 1984, *65,* 410–415.

Killen, M., Leviton, M., and Cahill, J. "Adolescent Reasoning About Drug Use." *Journal of Adolescent Research,* 1991, *6,* 336–356.

Killen, M., and Nucci, L. "Morality, Autonomy, and Social Conflict." In M. Killen and D. Hart (eds.), *Morality in Everyday Life: Developmental Perspectives.* New York: Cambridge University Press, 1995.

Killen, M., and Smetana, J. G. "Social Interactions in the Preschool Classroom and the Development of Young Children's Conceptions of Autonomy." Unpublished manuscript, University of Maryland, College Park, 1996.

Killen, M., and Sueyoshi, L. "Conflict Resolution in Japanese Social Interactions." *Early Education and Development,* 1995, *6,* 313–330.

Kuczynski, L., Kochanska, G., Radke-Yarrow, M., and Girnius-Brown, O. "A Developmental Interpretation of Young Children's Non-Compliance." *Developmental Psychology*, 1987, 23 (6), 799–806.

Mahler, M. S. *The Selected Papers of Margaret S. Mahler*, Vols. 1 and 2. Northvale, N.J.: Aronson, 1979.

Matas, L., Arend, R. A., and Sroufe, L. A. "Continuity of Adaptation in the Second Year: The Relationship Between Quality of Attachment and Later Competence." *Child Development*, 1978, 49, 547–556.

Miller, J. G., Bersoff, D. M., and Harwood, R. L. "Perceptions of Social Responsibilities in India and the United States: Moral Imperatives or Personal Decisions?" *Journal of Personality and Social Psychology*, 1990, 58, 33–47.

Nucci, L. "Social Development: Personal, Conventional, and Moral Concepts." Unpublished doctoral dissertation, University of California, Santa Cruz, 1977.

Nucci, L. "Conceptions of Personal Issues: A Domain Distinct from Moral or Societal Concepts." *Child Development*, 1981, 52, 114–121.

Nucci, L. "Morality and the Personal Sphere of Actions." In E. Reed, E. Turiel, and T. Brown (eds.), *Values and Knowledge*. Hillsdale, N.J.: Erlbaum, 1996.

Nucci, L., Camino, C., and Milnitsky-Sapiro, C. "Social Class Effects on Northeastern Brazilian Children's Conceptions of Areas of Personal Choice and Social Regulation." *Child Development*, 1996, 67, 1223–1242.

Nucci, L., Guerra, N., and Lee, J. Y. "Adolescent Judgments of the Personal, Prudential, and Normative Aspects of Drug Usage." *Developmental Psychology*, 1991, 27, 841–848.

Nucci, L., and Smetana, J. G. "Mothers' Concepts of Young Children's Areas of Personal Freedom." *Child Development*, 1996, 67, 1870–1886.

Nucci, L. P., and Weber, E. K. "Social Interactions in the Home and the Development of Young Children's Conceptions of the Personal." *Child Development*, 1995, 66, 1438–1452.

Piaget, J. *The Moral Judgment of the Child*. New York: Free Press, 1932.

Piaget, J. *The Equilibration of Cognitive Structures: The Central Problem of Intellectual Development*. (T. Brown and K. Thampy, trans.) Chicago: University of Chicago Press, 1985. (Originally published 1975.)

Shweder, R., Mahapatra, M., and Miller, J. "Culture and Moral Development." In J. Kagan and S. Lamb (eds.), *The Emergence of Morality in Young Children*. Chicago: University of Chicago Press, 1987.

Smetana, J. G. "Adolescents' and Parents' Conceptions of Parental Authority." *Child Development*, 1988a, 59, 321–335.

Smetana, J. G. "Concepts of Self and Social Convention: Adolescents' and Parents' Reasoning About Hypothetical and Actual Family Conflicts." In M. R. Gunnar and W. A. Collins (eds.), *Twenty-First Minnesota Symposium on Child Psychology: Development During the Transition to Adolescence*. Hillsdale, N.J.: Erlbaum, 1988b.

Smetana, J. G. "Adolescents' and Parents' Reasoning About Actual Family Conflict." *Child Development*, 1989, 60, 1052–1067.

Smetana, J. G. "Conflict and Coordination in Adolescent-Parent Relationships." In S. Shulman (ed.), *Close Relationships and Socioemotional Development*. Norwood, N.J.: Ablex, 1995a.

Smetana, J. G. "Parenting Styles and Conceptions of Parental Authority During Adolescence." *Child Development*, 1995b, 66, 299–316.

Smetana, J. G., and Asquith, P. "Adolescents' and Parents' Conceptions of Parental Authority and Adolescent Autonomy." *Child Development*, 1994, 65, 1143–1158.

Smetana, J. G., and Bitz, B. "Adolescents' Conceptions of Teachers' Authority and Its Relations to Rule Violations in School." *Child Development*, 1996, 67, 1153–1172.

Smetana, J. G., Bridgeman, D., and Turiel, E. "Differentiation of Domains and Prosocial Behavior." In D. Bridgeman (ed.), *The Nature of Prosocial Development: Interdisciplinary Theories and Strategies*. Orlando, Fla.: Academic Press, 1983.

Stern, D. *The Interpersonal World of the Infant: A View from Psychoanalysis and Developmental Psychology*. New York: Basic Books, 1985.

Stipek, D., Gralinski, J. H., and Kopp, C. B. "Self-Concept Development in the Toddler Years." *Developmental Psychology,* 1990, *26,* 972–977.

Tisak, M., and Tisak, J. "Children's Conceptions of Parental Authority, Friendship, and Sibling Relations." *Merrill-Palmer Quarterly,* 1990, *36,* 347–367.

Tisak, M., and Turiel, E. "Children's Conceptions of Moral and Prudential Rules." *Child Development,* 1984, *55,* 1030–1039.

Triandis, H. C. "Cross-Cultural Studies of Individualism and Collectivism." In J. J. Berman (eds.), *1989 Nebraska Symposium on Motivation.* Vol. 37: *Cross-Cultural Perspectives.* Lincoln: University of Nebraska Press, 1990.

Turiel, E. *The Development of Social Knowledge: Morality and Convention.* New York: Cambridge University Press, 1983.

Turiel, E. "Equality and Hierarchy: Conflict in Values." In E. S. Reed, E. Turiel, and T. Brown (eds.), *Values and Knowledge.* Hillsdale, N.J.: Erlbaum, 1996.

Vaughn, B. E., Kopp, C. B., and Krakow, J. B. "The Emergence and Consolidation of Self-Control from Eighteen to Thirty Months of Age: Normative Trends and Individual Differences." *Child Development,* 1984, *55,* 990–1004.

Wainryb, C., and Turiel, E. "Dominance, Subordination, and Concepts of Personal Entitlements in Cultural Contexts." *Child Development,* 1994, *65,* 1701–1722.

Weber, E. "Children's Understanding of Personal Prerogative in the Contrasting Contexts of Home and School." Unpublished manuscript, University of Wisconsin–Whitewater, 1996.

Yau, J., and Smetana, J. G. "Adolescent-Parent Conflict Among Chinese Adolescents in Hong Kong." *Child Development,* 1996, *67,* 1262–1275.

*LARRY P. NUCCI is professor of education and professor of psychology at the University of Illinois at Chicago.*

*MELANIE KILLEN is associate professor in the Department of Human Development and the Institute for Child Study at the University of Maryland, College Park.*

*JUDITH G. SMETANA is the Frederica Warner Professor of Education and Human Development at the University of Waterloo, Ontario, Canada.*

*Individual differences in affective dispositions and knowledge influence children's abilities to balance their own needs and goals with those of others without becoming aggressive.*

# Children's Conflict-Related Emotions: Implications for Morality and Autonomy

*William Arsenio, Sharon Cooperman*

In this chapter, we examine some of the emotional factors that influence children's understanding and behavior relative to conflicts and, consequently, the development of their autonomy as social agents. The principal focus is on children's actual emotional responses to various types of conflicts and, to a lesser degree, on their conceptions of conflict-related emotions. We begin with the view that children's emotional responses during conflicts and their understanding of those emotions are related to their ability to interact competently with peers. So, for example, children who are emotionally aversive during conflicts or who have atypical ideas about others' feelings may have fewer and poorer-quality opportunities than their peers to learn nonaggressive ways of resolving their conflicts. Ultimately, these problems with conflict resolution make it difficult for them to learn to negotiate with their peers and to develop the sorts of social and moral understanding that promote the development of an autonomous self.

## Conflicts, Morality, and Autonomy

Psychologists have long argued that conflicts provide a critical context for the development of both social and cognitive competencies. Piaget ([1975] 1985), in particular, described how conflicts and resulting states of disequilibrium lead children to abandon less adequate cognitive models and move toward increasingly sophisticated understandings of the world. In terms of social

Part of the research described in this chapter was supported by a grant to the first author from the National Institute of Mental Health (RO3 MH49753).

development, he proposed (1932) that interpersonal conflicts gradually lead children to understand the perspectives of others, and ultimately to construct a sense of reciprocity and fairness. The few studies conducted from this theoretical perspective do in fact suggest that social interaction promotes both cognitive (Bearison and Gass, 1979) and social-cognitive development (Damon and Killen, 1982).

Killen and Nucci (1995) have recently noted some important implications and potential limitations in the Piagetian perspective on the role of social conflict in children's development: "Moral autonomy in Piagetian theory is a developmental achievement reflecting a triumph of reason and reciprocity over egocentrism and respect for authority. From our perspective, Piaget's use of the term *autonomy* is limited because it leaves out legitimate concerns of the individual, that is nonmoral autonomous goals. We believe that a focus on the emergence of 'moral autonomy' ignores legitimate aspects of the nonmoral self that we think are important and have been overlooked" (p. 53). In other words, Piaget stressed that children's egocentric needs and desires come into conflict with the needs and desires of others, and the resulting conflicts (in combination with underlying cognitive changes) promote the development of role-taking, a sense of reciprocity, and an understanding and acceptance of the need for moral limits. For example, a sense of reciprocity emerges from this comment by an observed child, "If I just take her toy because I want it, then why can't she just take my toy whenever she wants it?" But what about conflicts in which victimization, ownership, and other moral limits are not so clearly at issue? What if two preschoolers are both playing in the block corner and they both reach for the last block, which will complete the separate buildings they are making?

As Killen and Nucci note, many conflicts do not involve overt victimization or other clearly moral issues but rather two children independently pursuing personal goals that happen to bring them into conflict. In these situations, children must still resolve a conflict between their own legitimate self-interests and those of others, and unlike the situation in acts involving moral victimization, simply subordinating one's needs and inhibiting behavior are neither morally necessary nor even desirable. In these *nonmoral* conflicts, then, children will need to coordinate their own needs and those of others in ways that promote a sense of personal agency and autonomy while also being responsive and fair. Thus conflicts are a critical interpersonal context for several related reasons. On the one hand, as Piaget suggested, they are important for establishing essential prescriptive limits on interpersonal behaviors, what is not permissible. On the other hand, however, they help to define an area of behavioral choice, or what Nucci has called the personal domain (Nucci, 1981; Nucci and Lee, 1993), in which personal goals and pursuits are more salient than overt prescriptive limits. Although many of children's actual conflicts may require them to coordinate both of these moral and personal elements, an exclusive focus on the moral domain fails to address the developmental importance of pursuing personal goals.

In this view, children's peer-peer conflicts are seen as allowing them to explore the boundaries between their own legitimate personal needs and goals and the legitimate needs and goals of others. Adults, however, also play a critical, if immediately less obvious, role in this process. At one level, adults must allow children the opportunity to work through at least some of their conflicts; too much adult intervention limits children's opportunities to learn how to resolve conflicts on their own without external assistance, consequently hindering the development of independence and autonomy. At the same time, adults must make essential judgments about the nature of children's conflicts. When conflicts involve victimization or potential harm to others, adults become less concerned about limiting children's opportunities than about addressing these moral infractions. Thus adults "make decisions to give priority to morality or autonomy depending on the nature of the consequences of the action" (Killen and Nucci, 1995, p. 65). When needed, adults may intervene in ways that promote conflict resolution by negotiation and understanding rather than by commands and sanctions (Killen, Breton, Ferguson, and Handler, 1994).

## Affective Influences on Children's Conflicts and Autonomy

In our own research, we begin with the view that children's conflicts and their understanding of conflict-related events are critical contexts for the development of both their moral understanding and their behavior, as well as for their pursuit of nonmoral goals. Furthermore, we believe that not all children are equally able to profit from their peer conflicts. Our particular interest is in the affective factors, ranging from emotional dispositions (such as moods and predominant emotional states) to children's understanding of emotions, that are likely to influence children's abilities to balance their own needs and goals with those of others. Some children, for example, may be less adept at recognizing the emotional cues of their peers, and they may also be more prone to becoming emotionally dysregulated during the course of such conflicts. Consequently, we would expect these children to exhibit more aggression with their peers, and to lose the developmental opportunities presented by conflicts. Taken one step further, as these behavioral patterns become more stable, it becomes increasingly difficult for these children to balance their desires, obligations, and personal goals, and ultimately, children's sense of personal autonomy as well as their perception of moral limits may become blurred, to the detriment of both.

In this view, nonaggressive conflicts assume a special importance for children's developing autonomy. To the extent that children's emotions and emotion-related abilities increase the likelihood of their conflicts becoming aggressive, however, they will be less likely to develop conflict resolution strategies that can promote nonmoral autonomous goals. Although a conflict may begin as two children's opposition to each other's legitimate goals (such as both needing that last special block to complete a project), once one child victimizes the other (such as by pushing her or him down and seizing the block), it becomes nearly impossible to coordinate the needs of the self with the needs of other people. In this sense, moral goals and nonmoral goals in children's conflicts have a complex relationship: although nonmoral conflicts are unique and promote different developmental goals than conflicts involving victimization, nonmoral opportunities emerge only when children refrain from resolving conflicts by victimization.

To date, much of our research on these issues has focused on children's conceptions of the emotional consequences of sociomoral events. As Harris (1985) noted, many of our behavioral decisions are influenced by "an anticipation of the way that we will feel in some future situation. A child's readiness to go to school, to brave the dentist, to seek out a new friend, or to run away from punishment is based on an appraisal of how he or she will feel when facing these situations" (p. 162). In other words, children's conceptions of situational affect—that is, of the links between specific situations and their associated affective outcomes—provide them with a means of anticipating and evaluating the emotional outcomes and consequences of a wide variety of social behaviors.

One finding with particular relevance for this chapter is the "happy victimizer" expectancy. Several studies (Arsenio and Lover, 1995; Dunn, Brown, and Maquire, 1995) have found that most young children expect moral victimizers to feel happy following acts of victimization that produce clear material gains, even when the victim and victimizers are close friends (Arsenio and Kramer, 1992). Furthermore, aggressive children (Lemerise, Scott, Diehl, and Bacher, 1996) and convicted adolescent offenders (Arsenio, Shea, and Sacks, 1995) are even more likely than their peers to expect moral victimizers to feel happy. If in fact many children expect victimization to produce positive emotions and material gains, this expectancy could undermine their efforts to resolve conflicts without resorting to moral transgressions.

In her influential review on children's conflicts, Shantz (1987) observed that "curiously little attention has been paid to children's arousal, to their anger or glee during adversative episodes. . . . Children's moods and emotions during and after conflicts are uncharted areas" (p. 300). Although this gap has been addressed somewhat in the past fifteen years (see especially Eisenberg and Garvey, 1981; Fabes and Eisenberg, 1992), we were concerned by how little we knew about children's conceptions of sociomoral emotions. Do young children actually display happiness in the course of some of their conflicts? What about the targets of these conflicts? What emotions do they display? Although our original interest was in the happy victimizer expectancy, it quickly became clear that more general studies were needed to characterize the nature and importance of children's emotions during conflicts, and to understand how these emotions affected both children's moral and nonmoral goals.

## Emotions, Conflicts, and Aggression
## During Preschoolers' Freeplay

With some of these issues in mind, Arsenio and Lover (1996) recently conducted a study to examine the relations among preschoolers' emotions, conflicts, and aggression during freeplay. Nonaggressive conflicts were defined as one child doing something to which a second child objected; such words as "refusing," "objecting," and "disagreeing" often were used to characterize such interactions. Aggressive conflicts were defined as one child aiming to hurt another child or his or her things, or attempting to verbally derogate another child (Shantz, 1987). One of our major goals was to examine whether children's emotions were connected differently with their aggressive and nonaggressive conflicts. Specifically, we expected that children's emotions would be more strongly linked with their aggression than with their nonaggressive conflicts, because intense emotions seem more likely to be associated with the adaptational failures implicit in aggressive acts than with less hostile attempts to resolve peer disputes.

Another goal involved examining the different contexts in which children's emotions emerge (that is, conflict-related emotions—emotions that emerge in both aggressive and nonaggressive conflict—and nonconflict, or "baseline," emotions). For example, in their work on the connections between preschoolers' emotions and prosocial behavior, Denham and her colleagues (Denham, 1986; Denham, McKinley, Couchoud, and Holt, 1990) found that children's general *moods* (emotions not associated with prosocial events) were among the strongest predictors of their prosocial reasoning and behavior. By contrast, when Arsenio and Killen (1996) assessed preschoolers' emotions during table play, they found that children's moods, or baseline nonconflict emotions, were unrelated to their conflict behavior, whereas their actual conflict-related emotions had multiple connections with their participation in nonaggressive conflicts (see also Fabes and Eisenberg, 1992).

At a theoretical level, it is important to know whether children's general baseline emotions are related to their behavior—for example, compared to their peers, are angry children more likely to become involved in conflicts? Alternatively, baseline emotions may be less predictive of negative behaviors than the emotions that children display during the actual course of their disputes: some children may seem no different emotionally from their peers until they become intensely emotional during their conflicts. Finally, there could also be obvious connections across these contexts, with some children being intensely emotional in both conflict and nonconflict settings. Although the overall connections between children's affective dispositions and their aggressive and nonaggressive conflicts are likely to be quite complex, it seemed important to begin to address some of these questions in our study.

The resulting study involved freeplay observations of thirty-seven preschoolers. Observers recorded several different aspects of children's conflict-related behaviors and naturally occurring emotions using a focal event sampling procedure (Altmann, 1974) in which children were observed for five randomly distributed ten-minute periods over six weeks. Children's happy, sad, angry, and (relatively rare) "other" emotional displays were assessed using an instrument expressly designed for the purpose of reliably coding "live action" emotions in naturalistic settings (Denham, 1986; Denham, McKinley, Couchoud, and Holt, 1990). All nonconflict emotions expressed by focal children were recorded, and in addition a separate record was made of the "peak" or predominant emotion that children (both the focal child and her or his conflict partner) displayed during conflicts. Consequently, it was possible to arrive at a measure of children's baseline emotions as well as their specific conflict emotions. A separate instrument was used to record several other aspects of conflicts, including the type of conflict (aggressive or nonaggressive), the child's conflict role (actor or recipient), and the length of the conflict. (The nature of the children's aggression, that is, whether it did or did not produce a clear material gain, was not recorded. As noted later, this may be an important issue when trying to interpret the meaning of children's aggression-related happiness.)

A total of seventy-six conflicts was observed, including twenty-nine aggressive conflicts and forty-four nonaggressive conflicts (thirty-four of thirty-seven children either initiated or were the target of at least one conflict). In the more than one thousand recorded emotional displays, the emotion children displayed most often (90 percent of the time) during nonconflict periods was happiness. By contrast, children displayed few emotions during conflicts, but when they did, the emotion was usually anger. Overall, two-thirds of the children's total number of angry displays occurred during the less than seventy-four minutes of conflict time, whereas the other third of their angry displays was spread over seventeen hundred minutes of nonconflict interactions. It is no surprise, then, that although conflicts "are rare and short, they should not be thought unimportant. . . . These events appear to have substantial affective meaning for the children involved" (Shantz, 1987, p. 286).

As expected, analyses also revealed some important connections between children's emotions and their conflict-related behaviors. Children who displayed more frequent nonconflict anger and a higher percentage of anger overall were more likely to become aggressive with their peers, whereas nonconflict emotions were unrelated to children's nonaggressive conflicts. In other words, hostile, angry moods were related to increased levels of aggression but not to increased levels of nonaggressive conflicts. A related pattern emerged for children's conflict-related moods. The percentage of children's anger during nonaggressive conflicts was unrelated to the frequency of any type of conflict behavior, in either aggressive or nonaggressive conflicts. Alternatively, children who displayed a higher percentage of both anger and happiness during their aggressive conflicts were more likely to initiate aggression. A final hierarchical regression revealed that nearly a quarter of the variance in children's initiation of aggression could be predicted by a combination of the percentage of their nonconflict anger, the percentage of their aggression-related anger, and the percentage of their aggression-related happiness ($r = .48$, $p < .05$). Interestingly, children's percentages of aggression-related happiness made a significant contribution even after accounting for their anger during aggression and baseline periods.

It appears, then, that preschoolers' emotions are more related to their aggressive behavior than to their nonaggressive-conflict behavior. In part this may be because children were also more intensely angry during aggressive conflicts than during their nonaggressive conflicts—that is, aggression may provide children with a more challenging emotional context. The other striking finding is that children frequently expressed happiness during aggression, and children who displayed higher percentages of aggression-related happiness were more likely to initiate aggression. These observational findings help to clarify why, as discussed earlier, preschoolers typically expect victimizers to feel happy following acts of victimization; in fact, initiators were happy during nearly one-third of the aggressive encounters in the study. (It must be noted, however, that we did not record whether aggressors obtained any direct material gain from their acts of victimization.) Most studies of children's conceptions of moral emotions have focused on victimization that produces concrete gains, and it is not known how children evaluate acts of victimization that do not involve such gains (see, however, Nunner-Winkler and Sodian, 1988, Experiment 2). In any case, it is clear that anger is not the only significant conflictual emotion.

Overall, these findings indicate that children who expressed a higher percentage of nonpositive moods, especially anger, were more likely to become aggressive than their less negative, less angry peers. It is also noteworthy that in both this study and in Arsenio and Killen (1996), conflict initiators who displayed a higher percentage of happiness were more likely to initiate conflicts and that, overall, negative emotions were associated with children's participation in conflicts. Collectively, these results suggest that children's hostile moods (both positive and negative) may also act to undermine the effective give-and-take needed for pursuing nonmoral personal goals.

One difficulty with this interpretation of the results, however, is that it assumes that children's emotions play a causal role in determining their conflictual interactions. Alternatively, it is also possible that children's conflictual problems are affecting their emotions or that there is a bidirectional relationship in which emotions are simultaneously both the cause and consequence of children's conflicts. For example, weak social-cognitive skills and lower levels of social competence may be related to preschoolers' conflictual behavior, and consequently, emotions may be a by-product as well as a direct cause of increased conflictual behavior.

Although establishing causality is always a complex task, it became clear to us that we needed more than just observational measures to understand the links between children's emotions and peer conflicts. Teachers and peers, for example, could also provide critical sources of additional information regarding the nature and causes of these connections. Teachers are in a unique position to witness children across a wide range of contexts within a time frame that usually lasts many months. Similarly, children can provide another, somewhat different close-up view of their peers' social behaviors through their sociometric ratings and nominations. Structured individual interviews with children were also needed to assess some of the social-cognitive abilities that are implicated in their emotions and conflict-related behavior. A larger, more comprehensive study was needed to examine the links among preschoolers' conflicts, their emotions, and the emergence of their autonomous goals.

## Emotions, Conflicts, and Children's Peer Acceptance

In a seminal early study, Cowen and his colleagues (Cowen and others, 1973) were interested in identifying childhood risk factors that predict serious maladjustment later in life. After following children for more than ten years using a variety of measures, they found that "peer judgment was, by far, the most sensitive predictor of later psychiatric difficulty" (p. 438). Since then, an extensive body of research has accumulated (Parker and Asher, 1987) that links children's peer status (that is, the various ratings of their acceptance or rejection by other children) with a variety of long-term outcomes, including aggression (Coie, Dodge, and Kupersmidt, 1990) and nonaggressive but disruptive behaviors (Coie, Dodge, and Coppotelli, 1982).

Consequently, in a subsequent study we decided to assess some of the general connections among children's sociometric ratings, their conflict-related behaviors and emotions, and their understanding of those emotions. We were especially interested in whether children's level of peer acceptance (that is, their tendency to be liked or disliked by their peers) was related to the nature of their peer conflicts and the emotions associated with those conflicts. Although there is an emerging interest in some of the emotional correlates of children's peer status and acceptance (for example, Hubbard and Coie, 1994), many of the overall connections between children's moods and conflict-related behaviors remain unclear. For example, Denham and colleagues (Denham, 1986; Denham, McKinley, Couchoud, and Holt, 1990) found that children's understanding of emotions was related to both their peer status and their prosocial behavior. We wondered whether children's understanding of emotions was also related to their peer acceptance and conflict-related behaviors. More specifically, would deficits in preschoolers' understanding of emotions be related to higher levels of aggressive behaviors, and consequently to fewer opportunities to pursue autonomous goals?

Another goal was to assess children's conflicts in more depth than we had in our previous research. For example, one important issue involved examining when and how adults and teachers intervene in children's conflicts (see Killen and Turiel, 1991). Adult intervention clearly limits children's opportunities to resolve their own conflicts and, as a result, may constrain the emergence of children's independence and autonomy. Yet adult intervention is obviously called for when children become aggressive or attempt to victimize their peers. One important question, then, is whether adults actually do intervene in different ways depending on the aggressive or nonaggressive nature of children's conflicts.

The remainder of this chapter is devoted to describing the methods and initial results of a study that was designed to provide more extensive information regarding the affective and sociometric factors that support the pursuit of nonmoral autonomous goals in some children while making it difficult for others to refrain from victimizing their peers.

**Methods.** The study included several types of measures including naturalistic observations of preschoolers' conflicts and emotions; two individually administered interviews of the preschoolers (a sociometric assessment and an assessment of their emotion-related knowledge); and several instruments completed by teachers to assess children's moods and emotional intensity, their aggressive behaviors, their peer popularity, and their social skills. Participants included fifty-one preschoolers (twenty-seven girls and twenty-four boys) between the ages of four and a half and five and a half from three preschool classrooms, and their teachers. All three classes were ethnically diverse, and more than half of the subjects were either Hispanic or African American. Most of the children were from lower- to middle-class economic backgrounds.

*Observations of Emotions and Conflicts.* A focal event sampling procedure (Altmann, 1974) was used to observe children for twelve 10-minute periods (120 minutes) randomly distributed over more than six months and over various times and activities in their preschool days. Children's happy, sad, angry, and (relatively rare) other emotional displays were assessed using the same instrument (Denham, 1986; Denham, McKinley, Couchoud, and Holt, 1990) and the procedures described earlier that were used for the Arsenio and Lover study (1996). A second observer recorded several aspects of all conflicts, again including the type of conflict (aggressive or nonaggressive), the child's role in an event, and length of the conflict. In addition, the conflict observer recorded a brief descriptive narrative for each conflict, using guidelines described in Hartup, Laursen, Stewart, and Eastenson (1988). Essentially, narratives included a brief, nonjudgmental, and sequential description of how the conflict started, what children did during the conflict, and how it ended.

*Children's Emotion Interview and Sociometric Ratings.* In addition to these observations, children participated in two individual interviews. In the emotion-related assessment, children were asked to label and recognize several basic emotions and to judge the probable emotional outcomes of several types of events that are familiar to preschoolers, ranging from acts of victimization and peer conflict to typically enjoyable events (adapted from Denham, 1986). Children also made peer assessments using the Asher, Singleton, Tinsley, and Hymel (1979) preschool picture sociometric procedure (see also Denham, McKinley, Couchoud, and Holt, 1990). Children rated each of their peers in terms of three categories of liking ("like a lot," "kinda like," and "do not like") by placing pictures of their classmates into one of three appropriately marked boxes.

*Teachers' Assessments.* Finally, at the end of the observational period, teachers completed four different assessments for each child in their class: the Dodge and Coie Aggression Scale (1987); an adaptation of Harter's Perceived Competence Scale for Children (1979), which yielded separate scores for children's popularity with their peers (for example, "has many friends") and their social competence and skills; a modification of the PANAS (Positive Affect and Negative Affect Scale) mood scale (see Clark and Watson, 1988), which produces scores for overall level of positive and negative affect; and the Emotional Intensity Scale, which assesses the intensity of children's positive and negative emotionality. (The last three instruments were kindly provided by Nancy Eisenberg. See Eisenberg and Garvey, 1981, and Fabes and Eisenberg, 1992, for more information on these instruments.)

**Results.** Children's sociometric ratings were used to assess peer acceptance. Children's ratings of whether they liked their peers were converted into a measure of peer acceptance based on the mean of all ratings for each particular child, and these mean scores were then converted to within-class z-scores to facilitate comparisons across classes. Three separate groups were formed containing seventeen subjects each: a low-accepted peer group, ranging from somewhat to strongly disliked by their peers (z-scores = −.48 to −1.78), an average group (neither particularly liked nor disliked [z-scores = −.47 to +.53]), and a high-accepted peer group (somewhat to strongly liked [z-scores = +.54 to +2.09]). All of the subsequent results are reported in terms of these three peer-acceptance groups—that is, how subsequent variables differed depending on each subject's inclusion in one of these three peer groups.

*Children's Nonconflict Emotions.* The three peer groups did not differ in the total number of their displays (that is, all of the nonconflict emotional displays taken together; mean per child per hour = 38.52). In other words, the groups did not differ in terms of general emotional expressiveness. Subsequent analyses revealed, however, that although the groups did not differ in the number of their happy (mean = 34.79) or sad displays (mean = 1.50), disliked children did express more anger than liked children (3.23 versus 1.25; disliked and average groups did not differ significantly: 3.23 versus 2.00). Furthermore, disliked children displayed a significantly lower percentage of happiness (87.0 percent versus 93.2 percent) and a higher percentage of anger (8.0 percent versus 3.5 percent) than liked children. Average and disliked children, however, did not differ in either their percentage of happiness (87.0 percent versus 90.6 percent) or their percentage of anger (8.0 percent versus 5.6 percent).

Overall, less-accepted children were not less emotionally expressive than their peers, but less-accepted children did display more total anger, as well as a higher percentage of anger and a lower percentage of happiness than liked children. Interestingly, this pattern (more anger and a higher percentage of anger) for less-accepted children resembles the pattern that emerged for more-aggressive children in the previous study (Arsenio and Lover, 1996). This similarity is probably related to the high overlap typically found between peer rejection and aggression—with aggression typically accounting for about one-half of the variance in peer rejection (Coie, Dodge, and Kupersmidt, 1990). In any case, it appears that children's nonconflict emotions have systematic and important connections with both their conflict-related behaviors and their levels of peer acceptance.

*Emotion-Understanding Interview.* Results from the emotion interview revealed that disliked children also had relative difficulties in their emotion-related abilities (including labeling and recognizing emotions and linking emotions and situations) in that disliked children had significantly lower total emotion-interview scores than either average or liked children (30.43, 33.94, and 33.80, respectively). The emotion deficits of disliked children are particularly important since similar deficits predicted lower levels of prosocial behavior and reasoning in previous studies (such as Denham, 1986). Similarly, these deficits are likely to make it more difficult for these children to be sensitive to the emotional cues of their peers during their conflictual interactions in ways that can promote children's pursuit of autonomous goals. In this regard, it is worth noting that children with lower emotional understanding scores in this study were also more likely to become physically aggressive with their peers $(r = -.57, p < .001)$.

*Teachers' Assessments.* Two teacher assessments provided additional evidence that disliked children's emotions differed in problematic ways from those of their more-liked peers. Specifically, teachers judged that disliked children were more likely to suffer negative moods and be more intense in their negative emotions than their peers. By contrast, no group differences emerged for either positive moods or positive intensity.

Teacher ratings of children's social competence and aggression also revealed a generally similar pattern of group differences. Within the social competence measure, teachers rated disliked children as having a lower level of social skills than either liked or average children. In addition, they rated disliked children as being less popular with their classmates than liked children. In judging aggression, teachers said that disliked children were more aggressive than average children, and although liked and average children did not differ significantly, the difference was in the expected direction.

In summary, a systematic and pervasive pattern of group differences emerged from the teachers' ratings, observations of children's nonconflict emotions, and observations of their emotion-related understanding. Compared to their peers, less-accepted preschoolers were more likely to display nonpositive emotions and especially anger, to have difficulties in recognizing and understanding emotions, to be rated as experiencing more intense negative moods, and to be seen as less popular and less socially skilled by their teachers. In addition, disliked children's very assignment to this group resulted from their peers' judgments that they were more problematic playmates than most other children. The next important question is whether these differences are also reflected in children's conflict-related behaviors. Do peer groups differ in how likely they are to become involved in conflicts? What about the nature of their conflicts—are there differences in the types of conflicts they get into? And finally, what are the implications of such conflict-related findings for children's ability to pursue their own autonomous goals?

*Children's Conflicts.* Children were observed participating in a total of 285 conflicts, including 172 nonaggressive conflicts and 113 conflicts involving aggression of one form or another. Although disliked children were involved in significantly more conflicts than either average or liked children (means = 6.6, 4.7, and 4.2, respectively, for disliked, average, and liked children), these results also differed depending on the aggressive or nonaggressive nature of the conflicts. The three groups did not differ in the number of their nonaggressive conflicts (3.1, 3.0, and 2.9, respectively, for disliked, average, and liked children), but disliked children were more likely to become aggressive (aggressive conflicts) than either their average or liked peers (3.5, 1.3, and 1.7).

Overall, disliked children were involved in 117 conflicts (47 percent non-aggressive, 53 percent aggressive); average children were involved in 83 conflicts (63 percent nonaggressive, 37 percent aggressive); and liked children were in 85 conflicts (69 percent nonaggressive and 31 percent aggressive).

Children's aggression was further divided into three separate categories: physical aggression (pushing, punching, and so on), verbal aggression (name-calling, teasing, and so on), and object-oriented aggression (for example, one child physically seizing an object belonging to another child). Disliked children were four times more likely than liked children (means = 1.5 versus .35) and twice as likely as average children (1.5 versus .7) to become physically aggressive. In addition, disliked children were almost twice as likely as either liked (1.3 versus .6) or average children (1.3 versus .8) to seize someone else's object. Finally, disliked children aggressed verbally more than average children (.7 versus .2), and somewhat more than liked children (.7 versus .35).

Overall, these results suggest that, as Killen and Nucci (1995) and others have observed, nonaggressive and aggressive conflicts present very different contexts for the development of children's peer relationships. Children's peer acceptance does not seem to be influenced by the frequency of their nonaggressive conflicts; rather, it is children's tendency to become aggressive in a variety of ways that is especially problematic. Consequently, children who are more likely to victimize their peers during conflicts will have proportionately fewer opportunities to engage in the sorts of conflict negotiations and resolutions that are essential for pursuing nonmoral autonomous goals.

At the same time, however, that disliked children had a lower percentage of nonaggressive conflicts than their more accepted peers, the actual number of their nonaggressive conflicts did not differ from the other groups (that is, disliked children were involved in more total conflicts, both aggressive and nonaggressive, and more aggressive conflicts, but not more nonaggressive conflicts than their peers). It could be argued that as long as disliked children have the same number of nonaggressive interactions as their peers, they will have sufficient opportunities to develop other important nonaggressive strategies for resolving conflicts, and ultimately to pursue their nonmoral personal goals. A subsequent analysis has important implications for this claim.

*Teachers' Interventions.*  A final set of analyses focused on teachers' interventions in children's conflicts. Namely, how often did teachers intervene in children's conflicts, and did their choice to intervene vary depending on the aggressive or nonaggressive nature of the conflict? An interesting pattern of results emerged. It was found that teachers did not differ in how often they intervened in three peer status groups' aggressive conflicts (25.9 percent, 22.0 percent, and 19.2 percent, respectively, for disliked, average, and liked children's conflicts). By contrast, for nonaggressive conflicts, teachers intervened more often for disliked peers (35.3 percent) than for either average (21.5 percent) or liked children (18.6 percent).

It appears that once a conflict involves aggression, teachers are not influenced by the level of a child's peer acceptance. In other words, moral infractions require intervention regardless of who is involved. (The relatively low percentage of teacher interventions into aggression is somewhat surprising, but in part this could be because aggressive conflicts are somewhat shorter than nonaggressive conflicts—mean = 2.57 turns for nonaggressive conflicts and 2.21 for aggressive conflicts—so that they are finished before teachers have a chance to intervene.) It may be that aggression requires intervention if the teacher is paying attention. By contrast, for nonaggressive conflicts, teachers were less likely to allow disliked children than to allow other children the opportunity to work through their conflicts. Perhaps this is because teachers realize that disliked children get into more aggressive conflicts than their peers, and teachers are afraid that unless they intervene, these conflicts have an increased probability of becoming aggressive. Unfortunately, this also means that disliked children will have fewer opportunities in which to develop the social skills and understanding that might eventually help them to pursue their personal goals in nonaggressive ways.

## Conclusion

In this chapter we have argued that not all children are able to profit equally from their peer conflicts. Our focus has been on individual differences in the affective factors that influence children's abilities to balance their own needs and goals with those of others without becoming aggressive. Results from several studies were summarized, and collectively these findings begin to shed some light on the connections among children's aggressive and nonaggressive conflicts and their affective dispositions and knowledge.

Most generally, preschoolers' naturally occurring emotional displays were found to have a number of systematic connections with their conflict-related behaviors. Children's tendency to display a high percentage of anger, in particular, was related to higher conflictual levels. In addition, teachers' ratings of children's moods and emotional intensity, as well as children's sociometric ratings, confirmed the connection between higher levels of negative emotions and increased risk for peer problems, including aggression. Some evidence also suggested that children display positive emotions when initiating conflicts, and that a higher percentage of such happiness is linked with more frequent conflict initiation (see Arsenio and Lover, 1995). It does appear, then, that children's hostile moods (both positive and negative) are likely to undermine the nonaggressive give-and-take needed for pursuing personal goals.

Another important finding is that children's emotion-related understanding is associated with their socially competent behavior. Children who were better able to recognize emotions and to understand situational emotions were less likely to become aggressive and were more accepted by their peers. In terms of children's emerging sense of autonomy, we would expect that children who are sensitive to the emotional cues of others not only are less likely to become aggressive but also will be more likely to resolve conflicts in ways that will allow them to pursue their own personal goals effectively (for instance, by using negotiation and providing peers with alternatives).

Finally, these results suggest that, as Killen and Nucci (1995) and others have observed, aggressive and nonaggressive conflicts present different contexts for the development of children's peer relationships. Children's emotions, for example, were more predictive of their aggressive behavior than of their nonaggressive behavior, and children's peer acceptance depended on how often they initiated aggression but not on their amount of involvement in nonaggressive conflicts. In other words, it is children's tendency to become aggressive rather than their involvement in nonaggressive conflicts that appears to be most problematic. Obviously, however, this does not mean that what children actually do during their nonaggressive conflicts is unimportant. Although not assessed in this chapter, other studies have shown that certain conflict resolution strategies are more likely than others to promote children's pursuit of autonomous goals (see Chapters One, Three, and Five). With this in mind, our subsequent analyses will focus on whether children's behavior during nonaggressive conflicts can help to explain why teachers intervened more often in the nonaggressive conflicts of disliked children than in those of other children.

## References

Altmann, J. "Observational Study of Behavior: Sampling Methods." *Behavior,* 1974, *49,* 227–267.

Arsenio, W., and Killen, M. "Preschoolers' Conflict-Related Emotions During Peer Disputes." *Early Education and Development,* 1996, 7, 43–57.

Arsenio, W., and Kramer, R. "Victimizers and Their Victims: Children's Conceptions of the Mixed Emotional Consequences of Victimization." *Child Development,* 1992, *63,* 915–927.

Arsenio, W., and Lover, A. "Children's Conceptions of Sociomoral Affect: Happy Victimizers, Mixed Emotions and Other Expectancies." In M. Killen and D. Hart (eds.), *Morality in Everyday Life: Developmental Perspectives.* New York: Cambridge University Press, 1995.

Arsenio, W., and Lover, A. "Emotions, Conflicts, and Aggression During Preschoolers' Freeplay." Unpublished manuscript, 1996.

Arsenio, W., Shea, T., and Sacks, B. "Delinquent and Typical Adolescents' Conceptions of Moral Emotions." Paper presented as part of the symposium "Developmental and Individual Differences in Affective Information Processing" at the biennial meeting of the Society for Research in Child Development, Indianapolis, Ind., March 1995.

Asher, S., Singleton, L., Tinsley, B., and Hymel, S. "A Reliable Sociometric Measure for Preschool Children." *Developmental Psychology,* 1979, *15,* 443–444.

Bearison, D., and Gass, S. "Hypothetical and Practical Reasoning: Children's Persuasive Appeals in Different Social Contexts." *Child Development,* 1979, *50,* 901–903.

Clark, L., and Watson, D. "Mood and the Mundane: Relations Between Daily Life Events and Self-Reported Mood." *Journal of Personality and Social Psychology,* 1988, *54,* 296–308.

Coie, J., Dodge, K., and Coppotelli, H. "Dimension and Types of Social Status: A Cross-Age Perspective." *Developmental Psychology,* 1982, *18,* 557–570.

Coie, J., Dodge, K., and Kupersmidt, J. "Peer Group Behavior and Social Status." In S. Asher and J. Coie (eds.), *Peer Rejection in Childhood.* New York: Cambridge University Press, 1990.

Cowen, E., Pederson, A., Babijian, H., Izzo, L., and Trost, M. "Long-Term Follow-Up of Early Detected Vulnerable Children." *Journal of Consulting and Clinical Psychology,* 1973, *41,* 438–446.

Damon, W., and Killen, M. "Peer Interaction and Processes of Change in Moral Reasoning." *Merrill-Palmer Quarterly,* 1982, *28,* 347–367.

Denham, S. "Social Cognition, Prosocial Behavior, and Emotion in Preschoolers: Contextual Validation." *Child Development,* 1986, *57,* 194–201.

Denham, S., McKinley, M., Couchoud, E., and Holt, R. "Emotional and Behavioral Predictors of Preschool Peer Ratings." *Child Development,* 1990, *61,* 1145–1162.

Dodge, K., and Coie, J. "Social-Information-Processing Factors in Reactive and Proactive Aggression in Children's Peer Groups." *Journal of Personality and Social Psychology,* 1987, *53,* 1146–1158.

Dunn, J., Brown, J., and Maquire, M. "The Development of Children's Moral Sensibility: Individual Differences and Emotion Understanding." *Development Psychology,* 1995, *31,* 649–659.

Eisenberg, A., and Garvey, C. "Children's Use of Verbal Strategies in Resolving Conflicts." *Discourse Processes,* 1981, *4,* 149–170.

Fabes, R., and Eisenberg, N. "Young Children's Coping with Interpersonal Stress." *Child Development,* 1992, *63,* 116–128.

Harris, P. L. "What Children Know About the Situations That Provoke Emotions." In M. Lewis and C. Saarni (eds.), *The Socialization of Emotion.* New York: Plenum, 1985.

Harter, S. *Perceived Competence Scale for Children: Manual.* Denver: University of Denver Press, 1979.

Hartup, W., Laursen, B., Stewart, M., and Eastenson, A. "Conflict and the Friendship Relations of Young Children." *Child Development,* 1988, *59,* 1590–1600.

Hubbard, J., and Coie, J. "Emotional Correlates of Social Competence in Children's Peer Relationships." *Merrill-Palmer Quarterly,* 1994, *40,* 1–20.

Killen, M., Breton, S., Ferguson, H., and Handler, K. "Preschoolers' Evaluations of Teacher Methods of Intervention in Social Transgressions." *Merrill-Palmer Quarterly,* 1994, *40,* 399–416.

Killen, M., and Nucci, L. "Morality, Autonomy, and Social Conflict." In M. Killen and D. Hart (eds.), *Morality in Everyday Life: Developmental Perspectives.* New York: Cambridge University Press, 1995.

Killen, M., and Turiel, E. "Conflict Resolution in Preschool Social Interactions." *Early Education and Development,* 1991, *2,* 240–255.

Lemerise, E., Scott, M., Diehl, D., and Bacher, S. "Understanding the Emotions of Victims and Victimizers: Developmental, Peer Acceptance, and Aggression Level Effects." Unpublished manuscript, 1996.

Nucci, L. "Conceptions of Personal Issues: A Domain Distinct from Moral or Societal Concepts." *Child Development,* 1981, *52,* 114–121.

Nucci, L., and Lee, J. Y. "Morality and Autonomy." In G. G. Noam and T. E. Wren (eds.), *The Moral Self.* Cambridge, Mass.: MIT Press, 1993.

Nunner-Winkler, G., and Sodian, B. Children's Understanding of Moral Emotions. *Child Development,* 1988, *59,* 1323–1338.

Parker, J. G., and Asher, S. R. "Peer Relations and Later Personal Adjustment: Are Low-Accepted Children at Risk?" *Psychological Bulletin,* 1987, *102,* 357–389.

Piaget, J. *The Moral Judgment of the Child.* New York: Free Press, 1932.

Piaget, J. *The Equilibration of Cognitive Structures: The Central Problem of Intellectual Development.* (T. Brown and K. Thampy, trans.) Chicago: University of Chicago Press, 1985. (Originally published 1975.)

Shantz, C. U. "Conflicts Between Children." *Child Development,* 1987, *58,* 283–305.

WILLIAM ARSENIO *is associate professor of psychology at Ferkauf Graduate School of Psychology, Albert Einstein College of Medicine, Yeshiva University, Bronx, New York.*

SHARON COOPERMAN *is a doctoral student at Ferkauf Graduate School of Psychology, Albert Einstein College of Medicine, Yeshiva University, Bronx, New York.*

*This chapter identifies parent-child collaboration as a primary influence on children's social competence with peers and tests this prediction with a large sample of mothers, fathers, and their six-year-old children. Results are consistent with the model, identifying fathers as likely contributors to differences in children's social competence, and suggesting a disproportionate parental influence on same-gender children.*

# Autonomy and Goal Attainment: Parenting, Gender, and Children's Social Competence

*Susan Crockenberg, Shelly Jackson, Adela M. Langrock*

Effective or socially competent behavior with peers signals the successful expansion of a child's relationships outside the family and sets the stage for further development in contexts with peers. Failure to develop competent peer behavior by the early school years has been linked to rejection by peers, poor self-esteem, and other types of maladjustment, including school failure (Kupersmidt, Coie, and Dodge, 1990; Parker and Asher, 1987). It is essential, therefore, to understand the origins of socially competent behavior if we wish to encourage its development and prevent maladjustment.

In this chapter, we present a model of the parental antecedents of young children's social competence with peers, briefly review relevant research, and present new data addressing the links between parent-child and child-peer relationships. We begin with a definition of what it means to be socially competent.

## Social Competence

Our concept of social competence is rooted in cultural beliefs about the importance of the individual, and hence in the necessity of maintaining individual

This research was supported by a grant from the W.T. Grant Foundation. We are grateful to Jane Nathan-Ailor, Patricia Murphy, and Christopher Pearson for their assistance in data collection and coding, and to Alan Howard and Taka Ashikaga for assistance with programming and statistical analyses. Correspondence regarding this chapter should be addressed to: Susan Crockenberg, Department of Psychology, John Dewey Hall, University of Vermont, Burlington, VT 05405.

autonomy (that is, freedom) to pursue goals. At the same time, it recognizes that individuals have competing goals that require them to accommodate to each other in the service of the broader principle of equity. The challenge is to achieve a balance that allows individuals to pursue personal goals while minimizing the impact of that pursuit on the opportunity of others to pursue their goals. Social competence is the achievement of this balance.

Socially competent adults and children pursue their goals while granting others sufficient autonomy (that is, freedom from constraint) to attain theirs. Although this orientation to self in relation to others is relevant to any social context, it is especially apparent during conflicts, which by definition occur when goals diverge. To illustrate: a socially competent child might suggest taking turns when there is disagreement about who will play with a desirable toy or who will go first in a game, or she might anticipate this conflict and suggest that the other child go first "this time." This is competent behavior because both children have the opportunity to attain individual goals, and mutual goal attainment contributes to the stability of peer relationships, both of which further individual development. In contrast, behavior that advances only one's own goals results in personal goal attainment at another's expense, whereas behavior that advances only another's goal does so at one's own expense. Either strategy limits individual goal attainment and jeopardizes peer relationships.

## Family Antecedents of Young Children's Social Competence

Parents are in a particularly powerful position to foster socially competent child behavior by virtue of their advanced social skills relative to children's and the early and repeated opportunities they have for interacting and resolving conflicts with their children. Unlike peer relationships, parent-child relationships are hierarchical; parents have more power vis-à-vis children by virtue of their greater experience and their role as socializing agents. Nevertheless, they can deploy this power in ways that either undermine or encourage their children's social competence. In our view, when parents pursue goals in ways that allow children sufficient autonomy to pursue theirs, they actively contribute to their children's developing social competence. We have labeled this behavior *collaborative*.

Like Baumrind's authoritative parents (1971), collaborative parents modulate their child's autonomy by giving reasons for their requests and prohibitions, by listening to their child's perspective, by attempting to persuade their child to comply rather than threatening adverse consequences for noncompliance, and by negotiating to achieve a more equitable solution from the child's point of view. The latter approach might involve delaying a task briefly (for example, to allow more time for play), reducing the scope of the task, or assisting with the task at the child's request. What is appropriate depends on the circumstances, the child's level of competence, and the nature of the competing goals. Firm enforcement, a key dimension of authoritative parenting, is not a central feature of collaborative parenting. Nevertheless, collaborative parents differ from parents who turn over control to their children (that is, permissive parents) by ensuring that their own goals are not neglected in the process of collaboration. It is this balance that fosters children's social competence.

The results of several studies are congruent with this conceptualization. Kochanska (1992) reported that mothers' use of suggestion with their two-year-olds predicted less frequent coercion and inarticulateness with peers at age five. Putallaz (1987) reported similarly that when mothers were agreeable during interactions, children were less disagreeable during play with peers. Fathers were not included in these studies, possibly because they spend less time with their young children than mothers (Parke, 1995) and thus are expected to have little influence on their development. One of the few studies of preschoolers' social competence to include fathers appears to confirm this view. Only maternal induction correlated with socially appropriate peer behavior, and only for girls (Hart, DeWolf, Wozniak, and Burts, 1992). There is evidence, however, that fathers' behavior in specific contexts (such as physical play) contributes to children's competence with peers. MacDonald and Parke (1984) reported that three- to four-year-old boys were popular with preschool classmates when fathers were physically playful but allowed their sons to regulate the pace and tempo of the interaction.

In addition, fathers may exert an increasing influence on social competence as children reach school age. Although on average fathers continue to spend less time with their children than mothers, Russell and Russell (1987) found that they were available to their six- and seven-year-old children 34.6 hours a week and initiated as much interaction with them as mothers when all three family members were present. Clearly, then, fathers have sufficient opportunity to influence their children's social development. Crockenberg and Lourie's (in press) data linking paternal behavior with six-year-olds' social competence are consistent with such an influence. Fathers' reasoning correlated positively with boys' use of negotiation during conflicts with peers and with ratings of girls' social competence. In contrast, mothers' guidance of two-year-olds predicted only girls' negotiation with peers at age six. This study and several others reviewed earlier report a greater parental influence within same-gender dyads. As Block (1976) suggested, fathers may make a concerted attempt to influence boys' behavior, or both boys and girls may adopt the behavior of the same-gender parent because they perceive it as consistent with their developing gender identity.

Although these findings are intriguing, generalizations about fathers' contributions to children's social competence are limited by small sample size and related power issues. It is also not reasonable to assume that maternal and paternal effects are independent, even when multicollinearity (the degree of correlation between measures of mothers' and fathers' behavior) is not an issue. Mothers and fathers may exert a cumulative influence on children's social competence when both behave collaboratively. Additionally, fathers' or mothers' collaborative behavior may moderate the potentially negative impact of the other parent's coercive or permissive behavior on children's social competence (Crockenberg, Lyons-Ruth, and Dickstein, 1993).

## Processes Linking Collaborative Parenting with Children's Social Competence

Collaborative parenting promotes children's social competence in several ways. Children observe parents using specific behaviors during conflicts, they practice those behaviors during interactions with parents, and they discover in doing so that the behaviors are effective in attaining goals (Ladd and Le Sieur, 1995). Children remember what worked with parents, expect it will be effective with others, and use similar strategies with peers (Pettit, Harrist, Bates, and Dodge, 1991).

When parents collaborate with children to resolve conflicts, children also learn that their own goal attainment is linked with the goal attainment of others. This learning has an affective as well as a cognitive component. Goal attainment is accompanied by positive emotion, a feeling of happiness or satisfaction. When attainment is mutual, this affective response becomes associated, through classical conditioning, with the goal attainment of others (Aronfreed, 1968). In effect, children develop a new goal, to further the goal attainment of others, as a result of interacting with collaborative parents.

Another way that collaborative parenting contributes to the development of social competence in children is by creating the conditions that promote internalization (that is, the adoption of the behavior as one's own). Erikson (1963) reasoned that children whose parents avoid overcontrol in the socialization process retain a sense of being autonomous agents within the constraints imposed by the social context. It follows that when these children comply with or accommodate to an adult, they do so with a degree of felt willingness or commitment (Crockenberg and Litman, 1990; Kochanska and Aksan, 1995), presumably because they attribute to themselves the decision to engage in the behavior. Kochanska and Aksan (1995) argue compellingly that this self-attribution is the basis of internalization, and they provide empirical data linking committed compliance to internalization of adult rules. When the motivation to engage in a behavior is internal, children are more likely to repeat it when adults are not present—for example, with peers.

Although we have focused on parental behavior that promotes children's social competence with peers, we also expect behaviors that focus disproportionately on either parents' or children's goals to undermine social competence, for some of the same reasons. It is widely documented that parental coercion correlates with and likely breeds child coercion by virtue of its strong modeling effect, the angry reaction it engenders, and the undermining of internalization processes (see Ladd and Le Sieur, 1995). Parental permissiveness is also expected to adversely impact children's social competence. Permissive parents fail to appropriately limit their children's autonomy at the point that the parents' and children's goals diverge. Parents' failure to advance their own goals teaches children to pursue their goals without regard to the goals of others, and at the same time deprives them of competent strategies for pursuing goals. As a consequence, children may learn that behaviors such as coercion are effective in attaining goals with parents (Patterson, 1982), and they may use more power assertion with peers (Gardner, 1989). If peers resist coercion, however, these children may imitate their permissive parents and demonstrate their lack of social competence by withdrawing from peer conflicts and giving up goals.

## Hypotheses

In the study presented here, we tested the following hypotheses about the collaborative, coercive, and permissive behavior of mothers and fathers in relation to children's social competence with peers:

Mothers' and fathers' collaborative behavior independently predicts children's social competence.

Effects on social competence are greater when both parents are collaborative with children.

Parental behavior that focuses on either parents' or children's goals at the expense of the other's goals (that is, coercive or permissive behavior) is associated with lower social competence.

Collaborative parenting moderates the effects of the other parent's coercion or permissiveness on children's social competence.

Associations between parenting and social competence will be stronger in same-gender dyads than in opposite-gender dyads.

## Method

**Participants.** The participants in this study were 164 mothers, fathers, and their five- and six-year-old children (83 boys and 81 girls) from two-parent Caucasian families. Seventy-one children had no siblings or were first-born. Mean age was thirty-eight years for fathers and thirty-five years for mothers; mean years of education were fifteen for fathers and mothers. Family income averaged $48,000 (ranging from $5,000 to $100,000). Couples had been married or living together for an average of eleven years (ranging from one to twenty-four years); all fathers had been actively involved as parents for at least one year.

**Procedures.** Data collection took place during two two-hour home visits, scheduled one to two weeks apart. At the first visit, one parent was interviewed using the Parent-Child Conflict Interview (PINT), completed the Child Behavior Checklist (CBCL) (Achenbach, 1991), and was observed interacting with his or her child on two conflict tasks. At the second visit, the same procedure was followed with the other parent, and the child was interviewed about peer conflicts using the Child-Peer Conflict Interview (CINT). The order of maternal and paternal interviews was counterbalanced.

*Parent-Child Conflict Interview.* The PINT is a narrative interview developed to assess the strategies mothers and fathers use to resolve actual parent-child conflicts, on the assumption that the strategies reported will be more ecologically valid than responses to hypothetical incidents (Crockenberg and Lourie, in press). It identifies important conflicts to equate parents' motivation to achieve compliance despite differences in conflict content.

The interviewer begins by defining conflict (disagreement) as a situation in which the parent wants the child to do something and the child objects. Then the parent rates a list of typical parent-child or family-specific conflicts (such as disagreements with siblings, bedtime, chores) on a scale from 1 (no disagreement) to 10 (extreme disagreement) and indicates how long each topic has been a source of disagreement. The three highest-rated disagreements are discussed in detail in the semistructured interview. The parent describes a specific incident in which each of these disagreements has occurred. Questions include the following: What do you usually do or say? How do you feel at the time of the conflict? What other strategies might you use in an effort to get your child to comply? At the end of each narrative, the interviewer asks if there is anything else the parent might do, and what he or she might do if the child does not comply.

All interviews were audiotaped, transcribed, and coded using twenty-five exhaustive and mutually exclusive conflict strategy categories. Percent-agreement reliability on 10 percent of the transcripts averaged .89 (ranging from .76 to 1.00) prior to beginning coding and remained at .85 midway through the project.

To reduce the number of variables, three composites were created for each parent by combining conceptually related categories and then inspecting the intercorrelations within and across composites: responsive reasoning as a measure of collaboration (empathy, affection, reinforcement, reasoning/explaining, inductive reasoning, proactive guidance, suggesting alternatives); giving up as a measure of permissiveness (give up and bribe); and coercion (withdrawal of privileges, verbal power assertion, physical power assertion for both parents, and physical punishment for fathers only). Correlations among the six parent variables were mainly significant but low (positively or negatively ranging from .18 to .24).

*Home Observation of Parent-Child Conflicts.* The home observation consisted of two conflict tasks: a standardized toy-pickup task and a task identified by the parent as something the child performs regularly but does not like to do (such as feeding a pet, making the bed, cleaning the table). The standardized toy-pickup task began when the observer gave the child a basket of attractive toys, helped remove all the toys from the basket, and played briefly with the child. Then the child played alone with the toys for ten minutes, at which point the parent asked the child to pick up the toys. When pickup was complete, the observer asked the parent to begin the second task.

The observer recorded parent-child interactions on audiotape and simultaneously described nonverbal behaviors on a separate channel. Observations averaged twenty minutes (ranging from ten to thirty minutes). Audiotapes were transcribed, then coded using a system adapted for this age group from Crockenberg and Litman (1990). Content codes were exhaustive and mutually exclusive, but could be assigned with any of the affect codes. Percent-agreement reliability between two coders on 10 percent of the transcripts averaged .92

(ranging from .75 to 1.00) prior to beginning coding and was reestablished midway through the project.

To control for differences in length of observations, the ratio of each strategy to the total number of strategies was calculated. The twenty-three ratio variables for mothers and fathers were factor analyzed using a varimax rotation. This yielded only one conceptually meaningful factor with an eigenvalue greater than 1, labeled *observed coercion* as seven negative strategies loaded positively ("tells to do," "high negative control," and "refuses to help") and three positive strategies loaded negatively ("acknowledge," "suggests/asks," and "praise"). Observed negotiation (suggesting an alternative that limits or alters the initial request) was included as an operational measure of collaboration. Only mothers' and fathers' coercion correlated significantly: $r(161) = .36, p < .01$.

*Child-Peer Conflict Interview.* The CINT draws on a procedure developed by Stein and Levine (1989) and adapted by Crockenberg and Lourie (in press) to assess the types of conflicts children have with peers, the strategies they employ to deal with those conflicts, and their feelings during conflicts. The interviewer begins by asking the child to identify conflicts they have with peers and to tell about a time when each identified conflict occurred—who was there, what the friend did, how the child felt, and what the friend did next— repeating this pattern until some type of resolution is achieved. The responses to peer behavior constitute children's strategies for resolving conflicts.

The interviews in our study were audiotaped, transcribed, and then coded using twenty-six behavioral categories adapted from Crockenberg and Lourie (in press). Categories reflected the degree to which children's behavior was directed toward "meeting own goals only" (coercion), "giving up own goals" (avoidance), or "meeting own goals with consideration for the other person" (competence), following Yeates, Schultz, and Selman (1991). Percent-agreement reliability between two coders based on 10 percent of the transcripts averaged .91 (ranging from .89 to 1.00) prior to beginning coding and was reestablished midway through the project.

Frequencies of each category of behavior were summed across the narratives for each child. When children used many strategies of each type (and frequencies of some strategies were low), they were assigned to a competence group based on their primary conflict strategies: competent-assertive children ($n = 51$, twenty-two boys and twenty-nine girls) used only competent strategies ("asks," "suggests a resolution," "reasons," "suggests a different game," and "refuses with reason"); coercive children ($n = 38$, twenty-one boys and seventeen girls) used only coercive strategies ("punishes," "uses physical force," "uses verbal threats," "gets mad," "excludes by sending home," and "asks authority figure who uses coercion"); and competent-coercive children ($n = 51$, twenty-three boys and twenty-eight girls) used at least one competent and one coercive strategy. Twenty-one children (thirteen boys and eight girls) could not be classified into any of the categories and were dropped from the analyses of the CINT data.

*Child Behavior Checklist.* Each parent completed the CBCL, a standardized measure of children's competencies, externalizing and internalizing symptoms, and behavioral problems (Achenbach, 1991). Two social competence measures derived from the CBCL are included in this report: the standard CBCL social competence scale (which includes items having to do with children's participation in organizations, their number and frequency of contacts with friends, and how well they get along with others) and a qualitative social competence variable, the average scores for items assessing the quality of the child's behavior with siblings, friends, and parents (item V1-A). For each relationship, parents rated the behavior of their child in comparison to other children his or her age as worse (scored as 1), about the same (scored as 2), or better (scored as 3). Mean standard social competence was 6.38, 6.19, and 6.57, and mean qualitative social competence was 2.30, 2.25, and 2.35, for all children, boys, and girls, respectively. Mother-rated standard and qualitative social competence correlated significantly: $r(126) = .48, p < .01$. In previous research, only qualitative social competence correlated with both parent-child and child-peer behavior (Crockenberg and Lourie, in press).

## Results

Three sets of hierarchical logistic and multiple regression analyses were conducted to test predicted associations between parental behavior and children's self-reported or parent-rated social competence. In the first set, each parent variable and each child gender were entered into the equation simultaneously, followed by their interaction, to test differential effects of parental behavior as a function of child gender. In the second set, pairs of significant parental predictors were entered with child gender to assess their independent prediction of social competence. In the third set, pairs of variables were entered with child gender, followed by all two-way interactions and then the three-way interaction, to test for cumulative and moderating effects. The latter analyses capitalized on chance as multiple pairs of parent variables were tested in separate analyses.

**Children's Self-Reported Social Competence.** Parents' ability to distinguish socially competent from less socially competent children (competent-assertive versus coercive, and competent-coercive versus coercive) was tested in separate logistic regressions. Results are presented in Table 3.1, and means for parent variables by competence group and child gender are presented in Table 3.2.

*Competent Parental Behavior.* Mothers' collaborative behavior predicted children's social competence: when mothers negotiated more, children were more likely to be competent-coercive than coercive; and when mothers reported more responsive reasoning, boys were more likely to be competent-assertive than coercive: $\chi^2(1, n = 44) = 7.94, p < .005$. There was also a cumulative effect of collaborative parenting on children's competence. Fathers' responsive reasoning interacted with mothers' negotiation and with child gender to predict social competence: $\beta = -.83, p < .05$. To interpret this interaction, four combinations of more and less collaborative behavior of mothers and fathers were created for boys and four for girls, for a total of eight groups, and

## Table 3.1.  Logistic Regressions Predicting
## CINT Social Competence from Parental Behavior

| | Estimate Coefficients ($\beta$) | | | |
| --- | --- | --- | --- | --- |
| | Mother | | Father | |
| | Competent-Assertive vs. Coercive | Competent-Coercive vs. Coercive | Competent-Assertive vs. Coercive | Competent-Coercive vs. Coercive |
| Responsive reasoning | .09 | .11 | .07 | .24 |
| Gender | .37 | −.01 | .42 | .26 |
| Reasoning × gender | −.70*** | −.28 | .22 | .04 |
| Observed negotiation | .22 | .39*** | .04 | .23 |
| Gender | .36 | .19 | .39 | −.03 |
| Negotiation × gender | −1.25 | −.18 | −.27 | −.11 |
| Reported coercion | −.12 | −.11 | −.17 | −.25** |
| Gender | .38 | .13 | .23 | .10 |
| Coercion × gender | .02 | −.05 | .18 | .63** |
| Observed coercion | −.03 | −.03 | −.01 | −.01 |
| Gender | .25 | .01 | .36 | .08 |
| Coercion × gender | .02 | .04 | .02 | .03 |
| Reported giving up | −.50** | −.33 | −.12 | −.49*** |
| Gender | .52 | .25 | .39 | .37 |
| Giving up × gender | −.23 | −.21 | −.42 | .30 |

Note: Positive betas for main effects indicate children more likely to be classified as competent.

*$p < .05$, **$p < .025$, ***$p < .01$.

the likelihood of being classified as competent-coercive or coercive was tested. The overall effect was significant—$\chi^2(7, n = 88) = 16.58$, $p < .02$—and between-group comparisons revealed that when both parents collaborated, children were more likely than when neither parent collaborated to be competent-coercive rather than coercive: $\chi^2(1, n = 31) = 10.78$, $p < .001$, and $\chi^2(1, n = 24) = 3.96$, $p < .05$, for boys and girls respectively. In addition, boys with two collaborative parents were more likely to be competent-coercive than boys with only collaborative fathers: $\chi^2(1, n = 21) = 7.29$, $p < .007$.

*Coercive and Permissive Parenting.*  Coercion and permissiveness were negatively associated with children's social competence. When fathers reported high coercion, children were more likely to be coercive than competent-coercive, although this effect was qualified by an interaction with child gender: fathers' coercion predicted child coercion for boys—$\chi^2(1, n = 47) = 10.98$, $p < .0005$—but not for girls. There were no main effects or interactions with child gender for mothers' coercion. In contrast, both parents' permissiveness predicted children's competence: mothers' permissiveness distinguished coercive from competent-assertive children, and fathers' permissiveness distinguished coercive from competent-coercive children.

*Independent and Moderating Effects.*  When pairs of significant parental behaviors were included simultaneously in regressions, each behavior remained

### Table 3.2. Means of Parental Behaviors for
### CINT Social Competence Groups by Child Gender

| | Competent-Assertive | | Coercive | | Competent-Coercive | |
|---|---|---|---|---|---|---|
| | Boys | Girls | Boys | Girls | Boys | Girls |
| Collaboration | | | | | | |
| Responsive reasoning | | | | | | |
| Mother | 4.91 | 4.45 | 3.14 | 5.41 | 3.96 | 5.39 |
| Father | 2.95 | 3.34 | 3.19 | 2.71 | 3.74 | 3.46 |
| Observed negotiation | | | | | | |
| Mother | 1.42 | 1.79 | 1.07 | 1.15 | 2.19 | 2.01 |
| Father | 1.33 | 1.50 | .94 | 1.65 | 2.00 | 2.25 |
| Coercion | | | | | | |
| Reported coercion | | | | | | |
| Mother | 3.45 | 2.86 | 3.48 | 3.65 | 3.39 | 2.86 |
| Father | 4.55 | 3.66 | 5.67 | 4.35 | 3.48 | 4.11 |
| Observed coercion | | | | | | |
| Mother | .46 | −5.44 | 4.53 | −1.34 | −1.98 | −3.21 |
| Father | −.31 | −4.69 | 1.49 | −3.13 | −2.57 | −2.81 |
| Permissiveness | | | | | | |
| Reported giving up | | | | | | |
| Mother | 1.18 | .97 | 1.48 | 1.94 | 1.22 | 1.21 |
| Father | 1.64 | 1.10 | 1.48 | 1.71 | .70 | .96 |

significant, as did the interactions after other significant main effects and inter-actions were entered.

Mothers' observed negotiation showed a trend to interact with fathers' reported coercion as a function of child gender: $\beta = .48$, $p < .06$. Comparisons of eight high/low maternal negotiation and paternal coercion groups by child gender demonstrated a significant overall effect: $\chi^2(7, n = 88) = 22.22$, $p < .002$. Specific comparisons revealed that boys were more likely to be competent-coercive when mothers were high on negotiation and fathers were low on coercion (that is, both parents were more competent) than when mothers were low on negotiation and fathers high on coercion (that is, both parents were less competent): $\chi^2(1, n = 26) = 19.07$, $p < .0001$. No buffering effect of competent maternal behavior on coercive paternal behavior was observed. To the contrary, having a coercive father reduced the positive effect of a collaborative mother on boys' social competence: $\chi^2(1, n = 21) = 8.02$, $p < .005$.

**CBCL Social Competence.** Although associations with parental behavior were tested for standard and qualitative social competence ratings, only results for the qualitative measure are reported due to space limitations and because only one of twenty correlations (main effects and parental behavior by gender interactions) was significant for the standard measure, no more than would be expected by chance. Results of the first set of hierarchical regressions are presented in Table 3.3.

*Collaborative Parenting.* Fathers' responsive reasoning predicted children's social competence. There were no main effects of mother's behavior or inter-

Table 3.3. Parental Predictors of Qualitative Social Competence

|  | Mother | | | Father | | |
|---|---|---|---|---|---|---|
|  | t | df | beta | t | df | beta |
| Responsive reasoning | .79 | 2, 152 | .06 | 1.96* | 2, 152 | .16 |
| Gender | 1.38 | 2, 152 | .11 | 1.69 | 2, 152 | .13 |
| Reasoning x gender | .07 | 3, 151 | .02 | −1.18 | 3, 151 | −.34 |
| Observed negotiation | .66 | 2, 151 | .05 | .17 | 2, 151 | .01 |
| Gender | 1.54 | 2, 151 | .12 | 1.41 | 2, 151 | .11 |
| Negotiation x gender | −.39 | 3, 150 | −.11 | −1.58 | 3, 150 | −.45 |
| Reported coercion | −1.22 | 2, 152 | −.10 | −2.74** | 2, 152 | −.22 |
| Gender | 1.47 | 2, 152 | .12 | 1.13 | 2, 152 | .09 |
| Coercion x gender | 1.69 | 3, 151 | .45 | .18 | 3, 151 | .05 |
| Observed coercion | −2.80** | 2, 151 | −.22 | −.57 | 2, 151 | −.05 |
| Gender | 1.22 | 2, 151 | .10 | 1.31 | 2, 151 | .11 |
| Coercion x gender | .28 | 3, 150 | .07 | .01 | 3, 150 | .00 |
| Reported giving up | −1.19 | 2, 152 | −.10 | −1.51 | 2, 152 | −.12 |
| Gender | 1.62 | 2, 152 | .13 | 1.65 | 2, 152 | .13 |
| Giving up x gender | .07 | 3, 151 | .02 | −2.28* | 3, 151 | −.59 |

*p < .05. **p < .01.

actions with child gender. However, when mothers' and fathers' negotiations were entered in the same equation, a significant three-way interaction was observed: $t(7, 145) = 2.03$, $p < .05$. Comparisons of children's social competence for each combination of high and low maternal and paternal negotiation by child gender revealed a buffering effect of fathers on boys; when mothers used less negotiation and fathers used more, boys were more socially competent than when both used less: $t(40) = 2.64$, $p < .025$.

*Coercive and Permissive Parental Behavior.* Mothers' observed and fathers' reported coercion negatively predicted children's social competence. Fathers' permissiveness showed a similar negative association in interaction with child gender; when fathers gave up control, girls were less socially competent: $t(75) = −2.52$, $p < .025$. Mothers' coercion interacted with their permissiveness for girls only, $t(3, 73) = −2.09$, $p < .05$. As shown in Figure 3.1, when mothers were coercive and gave up control, girls were less socially competent than when mothers were coercive but did not give up control.

*Independent and Moderating Effects.* When pairs of significant parental predictors were entered simultaneously, each predictor remained significant, as did the parental behavior when multiplied by child gender interactions.

Fathers' reported coercion and mothers' negotiation interacted to predict children's social competence: $t(4, 149) = 2.47$, $p < .025$. This was qualified, however, by a trend for a three-way interaction: $t(7, 146) = 1.94$, $p = .054$; mothers' negotiation interacted with fathers' coercion for girls only: $t(3, 72) = 3.19$, $p < .05$. As shown in Figure 3.2, mothers' negotiation buffered girls against the potentially negative impact of fathers' coercion on girls' social competence.

Figure 3.1.  The Interaction of Mothers' Reported Coercion
and Permissiveness on Social Competence, for Boys and Girls

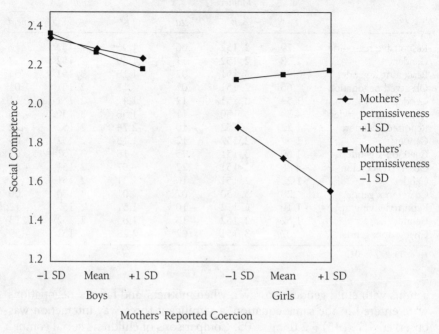

## Discussion

As predicted, when parents interacted with children collaboratively in ways
that allowed sufficient autonomy to attain goals in conflictual or potentially
conflictual situations, children behaved similarly during conflicts with peers,
and parents rated them as more socially competent. This prediction also was
not an artifact of collinearity: when pairs of significant predictors were entered
simultaneously, collaborative parenting continued to predict social competence. Thus it appears that children learn to balance attainment of their own
goals with those of peers when parents do so with them.

Evidence that when parents were coercive or permissive children were less
socially competent further supports the contention that regulation of autonomy between parents and children is central to the development of children's
social competence. It is particularly significant, in view of Baumrind's distinctions (1971) between authoritarian and permissive parenting, that the negative effect on social competence was apparent when parents allowed children
too much autonomy or control over outcomes, as well as when they restricted
children's autonomy unduly through their own excessive control. Moreover,
for girls, giving up control had a particularly detrimental effect on social competence when mothers were also highly coercive. This is consistent with Patterson's thesis (1982) that socially aggressive children have coercive parents

**Figure 3.2. The Interaction of Fathers' Reported Coercion and Mothers' Negotiation on Social Competence, for Boys and Girls**

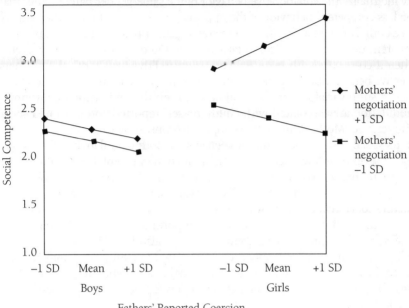

who back down when children escalate. Other data indicating main effects of both coercion and permissiveness on children's social competence suggest, however, that this combination of coercion and permissiveness is not the only type of parenting associated with less socially competent child behavior.

The data leave little doubt that both parents are implicated in the family process through which children become socially competent. In every instance in which fathers' behavior predicted children's social competence, the effect remained when significant maternal predictors were covaried. More important, there was a cumulative positive effect of having two competent parents: when girls and boys had two competent parents, they were significantly more likely to be socially competent and less likely to be coercive relative to children with two less competent parents.

Parents may have a disproportionate influence on six-year-old children of the same gender, although the data on this point are not entirely consistent. One intriguing possibility is that when the behavior of one parent is less competent, a competent same-gender parent may serve as a particularly effective buffer for the child. Two findings demonstrate this effect: (1) when mothers were less collaborative, having a collaborative father was associated with higher social competence ratings for boys but not for girls; and (2) when fathers were more coercive, having a collaborative mother was associated with higher social competence ratings for girls but not for boys. As suggested earlier, these effects may be a function of children's focus on gender as a key dimension for defining appropriate behavior at age six. Children may be more likely to use and possibly internalize the collaborative behavior of the same-gender parent rather than the less competent behavior of the opposite-gender parent when they experience both. Differential focusing on the same-gender parent may also explain the apparent undermining effect of fathers' coercion on boys' social competence when it co-occurs with maternal competence. Boys may adopt their fathers' coercive behavior because they define it as appropriate for themselves as males.

In sum, variations in parental behavior on the dimension of autonomy modulation are associated with children's self-reported and self-rated social competence. Mothers and fathers appear to contribute to differences in children's social competence, and these effects are both cumulative and moderating. In several instances, effects vary as a function of parental and child gender. To ignore this complexity is to fail to understand the intricacies of the family process through which children develop values, rules, and behaviors for conducting social relationships with peers.

These findings provide compelling support not only for including fathers in studies of children's social competence but also for doing so in ways that reflect the complexity of family processes related to family development. Failure to do so in the past may have contributed inadvertently to "mother blaming," the presumption that when children develop behavioral problems, their mothers are at fault (Caplan, 1989).

It is essential also to test the psychological processes that account for the transference of skills learned in families to children's relationships with peers. A central feature of the proposed model is that children not only learn competent strategies from collaborative parents but also develop the new goal of furthering the goal attainment of others. Information about children's emotional reactions to mutual goal attainment, as well as their expectations about their own goal attainment when others attain goals, would be useful in testing this aspect of the process.

## References

Achenbach, T. *Manual for the Child Behavior Checklist/4–18 and 1991 Profile*. Burlington: Department of Psychiatry, University of Vermont, 1991.

Aronfreed, J. *Conduct and Conscience*. Orlando, Fla.: Academic Press, 1968.

Baumrind, D. "Current Patterns of Parental Authority." *Developmental Psychology Monograph*, 1971, *4* (1), 1–103.

Block, J. H. "Issues, Problems, and Pitfalls in Assessing Sex Differences: A Critical Review of the Psychology of Sex Differences." *Merrill-Palmer Quarterly*, 1976, 22, 283–308.

Caplan, P. *Don't Blame Mother: Mending the Mother-Daughter Relationship*. New York: Harper-Collins, 1989.

Crockenberg, S., and Litman, C. "Autonomy as Competence in Two-Year-Olds: Maternal Correlates of Child Defiance, Compliance, and Self-Assertion." *Developmental Psychology*, 1990, *26*, 961–971.

Crockenberg, S., and Lourie, A. E. "Parents' Conflict Strategies with Children and Children's Conflict Strategies with Peers." *Merrill-Palmer Quarterly*, in press.

Crockenberg, S., Lyons-Ruth, K., and Dickstein, S. "The Family Context of Infant Mental Health: Infant Development in Multiple Family Relationships." In C. H. Zeanah, Jr. (ed.), *Handbook of Infant Mental Health*. New York: Guilford Press, 1993.

Erikson, E. *Childhood and Society*. New York: Norton, 1963.

Gardner, F.E.M. "Inconsistent Parenting: Is There Evidence for a Link with Children's Conduct Problems?" *Journal of Abnormal Child Psychology*, 1989, *17*, 223–233.

Hart, C. H., DeWolf, D. M., Wozniak, P., and Burts, D. C. "Maternal and Paternal Disciplinary Styles: Relations with Preschoolers' Playground Behavioral Orientations and Peer Status." *Child Development*, 1992, *63*, 879–892.

Kochanska, G. "Children's Interpersonal Influence with Mothers and Peers." *Developmental Psychology*, 1992, *28* (3), 491–499.

Kochanska, G., and Aksan, N. "Mother-Child Mutually Positive Affect: The Quality of Child Compliance to Requests and Prohibitions, and Maternal Control as Correlates of Early Internalization." *Child Development*, 1995, *66*, 236–254.

Kupersmidt, J. B., Coie, J. D., and Dodge, K. A. "The Role of Poor Peer Relationships in the Development of Disorder." In S. R. Asher and J. D. Coie (eds.), *Peer Rejection in Childhood*. New York: Cambridge University Press, 1990.

Ladd, G. W., and Le Sieur, K. D. "Parents and Children's Peer Relationships." In M. H. Bornstein (ed.), *Handbook of Parenting, Vol. 4: Applied and Practical Parenting*. Hillsdale, N.J.: Erlbaum, 1995.

MacDonald, K. B., and Parke, R. D. "Bridging the Gap: Parent-Child Play Interaction and Interactive Competence." *Child Development*, 1984, *55*, 1265–1277.

Parke, R. D. "Fathers and Families." In M. H. Bornstein (ed.), *Handbook of Parenting*. Vol. 3: *Status and Social Conditions of Parenting*. Hillsdale, N.J.: Erlbaum, 1995.

Parker, J. G., and Asher, S. R. "Peer Relations and Later Personal Adjustment: Are Low-Accepted Children at Risk?" *Psychological Bulletin*, 1987, *102*, 357–389.

Patterson, G. R. *A Social Learning Approach to Family Intervention*. Vol. 3: *Coercive Family Process*. Eugene, Oreg.: Castalia, 1982.

Pettit, G. S., Harrist, A. W., Bates, J. E., and Dodge, K. A. "Family Interaction, Social Cognition, and Children's Subsequent Relationships with Peers at Kindergarten." *Journal of Social and Personal Relationships*, 1991, *8*, 383–402.

Putallaz, M. "Maternal Behavior and Children's Sociometric Status." *Child Development*, 1987, *58*, 324–340.

Russell, G., and Russell, A. "Mother-Child and Father-Child Relationships in Middle-Childhood." *Child Development*, 1987, *58*, 1573–1585.

Stein, N. L., and Levine, L. J. "The Causal Organization of Emotional Knowledge: A Developmental Study." *Cognition and Emotion*, 1989, *3* (4), 343–378.

Yeates, K. O., Schultz, L. H., and Selman, R. L. "The Development of Interpersonal Negotiation Strategies in Thought and Action: A Social-Cognitive Link to Behavioral Adjustment and Social Status." *Merrill-Palmer Quarterly*, 1991, *37*, 369–406.

*SUSAN CROCKENBERG is professor of psychology at the University of Vermont.*

*SHELLY JACKSON recently completed her Ph.D. at the University of Vermont and is currently a postdoctoral fellow at the University of Nebraska–Lincoln.*

*ADELA M. LANGROCK is completing her Ph.D. at the University of Chicago and has been working with Susan Crockenberg at the University of Vermont.*

*Children need adult guidance in order to learn the culturally acceptable ways of resolving their conflicts. We describe how preschool teachers help children through dialogue to negotiate their perspectives.*

# The Role of Teacher Assistance in Children's Construction of Intersubjectivity During Conflict Resolution

*Artin Göncü, Virginia Cannella*

Many developmental theorists claim that conflict plays a significant role in children's development (Shantz, 1987). However, research efforts to understand the nature of children's conflicts have been sparse (Grimshaw, 1990; Shantz and Hartup, 1992). Some scholars state that the relative lack of research on children's conflicts may be a reflection of the prominent value in the United States that neither experiencing nor talking about conflict is desirable (Valsiner and Cairns, 1992).

Whatever the reason, there have been even fewer efforts to understand the role of adult involvement in children's conflicts. A small number of scholars have examined whether or not parental intervention (Bryant and Crockenberg, 1980; Ross and Conant, 1992) or teacher intervention (Killen and Turiel, 1991) assists children in resolving their conflicts. However, how an adult assists children in resolving their interpersonal conflicts remains largely unknown. This is especially true in the field of early childhood education. What is currently known about teacher assistance with children's conflicts is mostly limited to

The first author's work was supported by the Spencer Foundation during the writing of this chapter. We acknowledge Ageliki Nicolopoulou and Joe Becker for engaging in discussions with us in the formulation of ideas reported in this chapter. Special thanks are extended to Ute Tuermer for her help in identification of the conflict segments in the transcripts. Reprint requests should be sent to Artin Göncü, Department of Educational Psychology, University of Illinois at Chicago, Chicago, IL 60607.

daily practice in the classroom. Scholarly descriptions of teacher-child collaboration in conflict resolution are lacking. In our effort to fill this gap, we propose a model of teacher assistance in children's conflict resolution.

To achieve this goal, we first present the role of conflict in the developmental theories that guided our work. Then we discuss the two questions we address in our model of the role of teacher assistance in children's conflicts: When does teacher assistance in children's conflicts become necessary? and How does a teacher assist children to resolve their conflicts? In the present paper, we focus more on the second question and argue that assisting children in conflict resolution requires conceptualizing conflict as a problem. We maintain that resolution of children's conflicts is guided by cultural values that regulate children's interactions. A preschool teacher imparts such values to children by engaging in implicit or explicit communication with children in the effort to lead them toward a resolution of their conflict. We end with some suggestions for future research.

## Conflict Resolution in Developmental Theory: Piaget and Vygotsky

We define interpersonal conflict broadly as disagreements or oppositional interaction between individual children or groups of children. The oppositional interaction emerges when one party's effort to influence another party or parties results in refusal (Shantz, 1987; Laursen and Hartup, 1989). For example, when a child approaches a group of children to play with them and the group rejects the child's overtures, a conflictful interaction emerges.

Conflicts emerging from children's interactions with their peers have received notable theoretical attention. For example, Piaget (1932) conceptualized children's interpersonal conflict as a force essential for their development. According to Piaget, preschool children's conflicts with their peers enable them to overcome their egocentrism. In a conflictful interaction, the disequilibrium caused by the difference of opinions leads children to take into account one another's perspectives. As a result, children come to understand that their peers may have different thoughts and feelings about the problem in question (DeVries and Göncü, 1987; Selman, Schorin, Stone, and Phelps, 1983).

Piaget claimed that adults should cooperate with children during conflict resolution in order to enable the children to understand one another's perspective. For Piaget, cooperation with children means guiding them to regulate their interaction not by telling them what to do but by encouraging them to discover how they are affected by one another's actions. In Piaget's own words, this is possible only if the adult reduces her power and "becomes a comrade to the children" (1932, p. 364). Adult guidance provided in the position of an equal enables children to freely exchange ideas, resulting in the development of autonomy, described as self-government in relation to other people.

We acknowledge that Piaget's theory guided us in understanding the role of conflict in the decline of children's egocentrism. Also, in principle we agree with Piaget that cooperation with children leads them toward perspective taking and, ideally, toward the resolution of their conflict. However, we believe that Piaget's ideas need extension on three grounds. First, increasing cross-cultural evidence suggests that the meaning of cooperation and autonomy may vary depending on the cultural or school community in which children grow up (Greenfield and Cocking, 1994; Rogoff, Mistry, Göncü, and Mosier, 1993; Shweder, 1990). Therefore, we present our Piaget-inspired notion of adult-child cooperation as one of many possible ways of working with children. Second, and corollary to the first suggestion, we proffer that sometimes when guiding children's interactions the teacher's cultural values may lead her to exert her adult power. Further, we believe that even when the teacher acts as if she is a peer of equal status to children, she is still in control of her interaction with them. Third, Piaget's theory does not address the communicative processes by which the adult assists children in conflict resolution. In our effort to develop a cultural framework for analyzing the communication of conflict resolution, we draw from the theory of Vygotsky and the theory of intersubjectivity.

Vygotsky (1978) conceptualizes the development of an individual as a process of acquiring knowledge and understandings valued by the adults' culture (Cole, 1989; Rogoff, 1990; Wertsch, 1985a, 1985b). According to Vygotsky, acquisition of knowledge takes place in the *zone of proximal development*, where children can function only with the assistance of partners who are more competent than themselves.[1] During their interaction in the zone of proximal development, adults progressively make their knowledge available to children, and children gradually learn to use adults' understanding to transform their own existing understandings. As a result, joint functioning in the zone of proximal development becomes a part of children's own internal understanding of the knowledge valued by the adults (Göncü and Becker, 1992). This independent functioning emerging from the child's collaboration with the adults describes the child's actual developmental level.

Some scholars refer to the interactive process in which adults make available to children their understanding, and children learn to use such understanding to construct intersubjectivity (Göncü, 1993; Rommetveit, 1979; Wertsch, 1984; Rogoff, 1990). According to Trevarthen (1979, 1988), construction of intersubjectivity or shared understanding among the participants of an activity is achieved through recognition and coordination of intentions in communication. Such coordination is accomplished by two activities that occur simultaneously. These are adoption of a shared focus of attention and agreements on the nature of communication. A shared focus of attention serves as a starting point for communication and enables participants to expand their existing knowledge and understanding to new situations. Agreements on the nature of communication enable the participants to adopt the appropriate course of action in their interaction.

Research following Vygotsky has shown that when children are confronted with a problem such as classifying objects (Göncü and Rogoff, 1991) or solving puzzles (Wertsch, 1984), they need guidance to learn the solution that is valued by the culture as appropriate. In a similar vein, we believe that conflict resolution is a problem-solving activity similar to solving a classification problem and requires adult guidance. It is the responsibility of adults to make available to children, during their joint effort to resolve children's conflicts, culturally valued skills that children can use later without the adult's assistance.

From the Vygotskyan point of view, adult assistance can take many forms depending on a host of factors. For example, adult-child interactions vary in different types of activities (such as play or work) and in different means of communication are employed (such as verbal or nonverbal). Additionally, in different types of power relations the interactions vary (such as when the adult is in a peer role with equal power to children or when the adult has power over the child).

As we have indicated, Piaget and Vygotsky offered complementary views that guided us in the construction of our model of teacher assistance in children's conflict resolution. In particular, Piaget viewed interpersonal conflict as an essential force in children's development without including culture as part of his theoretical stance. Vygotsky did not focus on conflict in his theory, although he viewed culture represented by adults as the guiding force for children's development. In our model, we integrate Vygotsky's stance on the role of culture with Piaget's proposal on adult-child cooperation as one of many possible cultural models of adult assistance in children's conflict resolution.

We define culture or community as a group of people with a local organization and common values and practices (Laboratory of Comparative Human Cognition, 1983; Rogoff, Mistry, Göncü, and Mosier, 1993). The specific features of a given culture that differentiate it from others may have been passed on from a previous generation, or they may have been constructed anew by its members (Tudge, Lee, and Putnam, 1995). In what follows, we present the attitudes about children's development and education shared and promoted by the culture of a particular community of classroom teachers, parents, and university personnel involved in an urban and inner-city school. We elaborate the features of this culture as it relates to how teachers assist children in resolving their conflicts. We outline a practice based on the value that a preschool teacher should aim to assist children in negotiating their perspectives through dialogue by recognizing and supporting each child's need for self-expression. To do so, we extend Piaget's and Vygotsky's theories in our analyses of the role relations between teachers and children during children's conflict resolution. Further, we illustrate how teachers assist children in their construction of intersubjectivity to reach a resolution of their conflict.

## Teacher Assistance in Conflict Resolution

Our insight in response to our first question—When does a teacher offer assistance with children's conflict?—is motivated by how Piaget and Vygotsky conceptualized the goal of development. Both men viewed the goal of development similarly, as attaining autonomy (Piaget, 1932) or independent functioning (Vygotsky, 1978). Building on their ideas and on pedagogical expectations in the United States, we feel that it is appropriate for a preschool teacher to provide children with opportunities to solve their conflicts on their own without the assistance of a teacher. Children's voices coming from the existing research indicate that they are in agreement with these developmental theorists: they do not often require adult intervention in finding a solution to their conflicts (Shantz, 1987; Genishi and di Paolo, 1982; Laursen and Hartup, 1989).

When, then, is teacher assistance justified? Realistically, this is a difficult question to answer. The judgment of each teacher is influenced by such factors as daily circumstances, the individual children involved, and the culture of children and teachers. Sometimes a teacher may have to intervene even if children resolve their conflict on their own. For example, when a child is unfairly prevented by the group from using a play material and succumbs to the group's decision, a teacher may intervene to help all the children involved to understand that the solution is not acceptable. Teaching children about fairness may require rejecting their solution even if all the children involved appear contented with their own solution.

There are times, however, when the teacher may offer assistance only in response to children's request. For example, when two children are in a conflict about who is bigger, the teacher may offer assistance only if the children solicit her opinion, provided that the children's interaction does not involve aggression.

The question of when and how a preschool teacher should intervene in children's conflicts has not been addressed in theory, although some general guidelines have been offered (Derman-Sparks and the ABC Task Force, 1989; DeVries and Zan, 1994; Grusec and Goodnow, 1994). In a similar vein, we are not certain about when preschoolers require teacher intervention in their conflicts. We leave these questions to be explored in future work. For us, a more immediate question was how does a teacher assist children after children have requested the teacher's assistance? To address this question, we made an effort to build a model of teacher-child communication during conflict resolution.

## How Does a Teacher Assist Children in Constructing Intersubjectivity in Conflict Resolution?

Constructing intersubjectivity is an evolving dialogical process in which partners negotiate their individual understandings to reach a shared understanding. The approach that is most suitable to analyzing construction of intersubjectivity is sociolinguistic (Corsaro and Rizzo, 1990; Garvey and Shantz, 1992). The sociolinguistic approach emphasizes analysis of interaction in terms of conversational turns, allowing identification of the contribution of each individual to the construction of intersubjectivity in dialogue.

To illustrate the role of teacher assistance in children's construction of intersubjectivity, we make available to the reader actual linguistic interactions between teachers and children, to inform the reader about the bases of our interpretations and to enable possible reinterpretations of our data. Also, the illustrations can be used to develop coding categories for future quantitative hypothesis testing research.

The illustrations included in this chapter come from data collected for a larger project on cultural differences in young children's play. Fourteen African American children were videotaped as they freely engaged in activities of their own choice in a state prekindergarten program. The second author of this chapter served as the head teacher. The other adults who were regularly present in the classroom were an assistant teacher and a parent volunteer.

Children's conflicts and teacher assistance were not thought of as part of the study at the time of the data collection, and the teachers did not know that their interactions would be used in the present project for illustrative purposes. We thus feel confident that the illustrations represent how the teachers interact with children during conflict resolution on a daily basis.

Our conceptualization of conflict as a problem, the solution of which results in perspective taking, led us to structure the communication of conflict resolution in three phases: identification of the conflict, concern with the emotional effect of the conflict on the participants, and working toward a solution. We focused on teachers' assistance in children's construction of intersubjectivity in these three phases.

**Identification of the Conflict.** The teacher's involvement begins when children request help with an ongoing conflict. It is the cultural value of the teacher to interpret any approach as a request for guidance in the zone of proximal development for all the children. Guidance for the group is necessary even if some of the children have a justifiable stance, with which the teacher agrees, toward the substance of the conflict. These children may have other related needs, such as to learn to communicate their ideas more effectively, and to learn to assist the peers with whom they have the conflict. Thus we believe that the teacher's guidance should begin almost invariably by making sure that all the parties involved in the conflict are present to assume their responsibility in working toward a solution. Clearly, our approach does not preclude having further separate conversations with individual children when necessary.

The cultural value that guides our practice involves interaction in which the teacher begins the conversation by questioning children about what happened and why it happened. This leads simultaneously to the adoption of a shared focus of attention and the making of decisions about the nature of communication during conflict. With respect to the former, the children have to reconstruct the sequence of their interaction jointly and come to an agreement about the conflict as they inform the teacher of what happened. With respect to making decisions about the communication of conflict, the teacher's questioning about what happened gives two related messages to children. First, the participants need to establish what the problem is before any further communicative steps can be taken. Second, the teacher offers assistance in a question-

and-answer mode of communication in which the teacher questions and the children answer about what happened. The following exchange illustrates how the teacher and children jointly identify the problem in the course of a specific question-and-answer sequence.

Before the teacher's assistance is requested, Mark goes over to a table where several boys, including Tommy and Tony, are playing with pretend paper money. Mark tries to join them, and the other boys' refusal of Mark's request results in conflict.

MARK:  Can I play with you, Tony?
TONY  [*Shakes his head to mean no*].
[*Mark takes Tony's pretend money from the table. Tony turns around and tries to get it back.*]
TOMMY:  [*To Mark*] Give it back, you little [inaudible].
[*Tommy gets up, runs over to Mark, and starts choking him. Mark begins to cry and Tommy lets him go. Mark runs to the teacher as he continues to cry.*]

The teacher seeks information about the conflict and helps the children restate the problem by asking questions, which the children answer.

TEACHER:  What happened? [*She takes Mark back to where the other boys are. Mark tries to tell what happened.*]
MARK:  I say can I play; he said no.
TEACHER:  What happened, Mark?
MARK:  I say can I play, he said yeah, but start fightin' on me.
TEACHER:  He put what on you?
MARK:  He threw a fight on me.
TOMMY:  No, he took that money from Tony and then Tony said put it back here, put it back.
TEACHER:  And then what happened?
TOMMY:  And he didn't give it back to Tony and Tony had got up.
TEACHER:  So what happened?
TOMMY:  He all started crying, like a little crybaby.
TEACHER:  No [*disapproving the name-calling*].
MARK:  [*Crying*] He called me stupid, too.
[*Tommy tries to avoid the interaction by starting to talk to another boy nearby.*]

At this point, the teacher is relying on the children's narrative, Tommy's name-calling, and his attempt to avoid the interaction. She is accepting that the children expressed in their conversation with her the nature of their conflict: rejecting Mark from the group play, not tolerating Mark's taking of pretend money, a possible fight, and name-calling. After having adopted a shared focus of attention, and because of her desire to keep children in the interaction, the teacher moves on to the next stage in conflict resolution.

**Concerns About the Emotional Effect on Participants.** The second area in which children need guidance in working out their differences involves expressing how the conflict affects them. The discourse about children's feelings serve two related purposes: first, children inform one another about their feelings; and second, expression of feelings prepares the ground for deciding on the possible solutions for the conflict.

We identified two ways in which the teacher assists children in constructing intersubjectivity with reference to their affect. One of these ways is to ask children directly to state how they feel about what happened. For example, in the conflict between Tommy and Mark the teacher thinks it is essential to address Mark's hurt immediately, and she focuses on that part of their multifaceted conflict. The cultural value the teacher wants to convey to the children as a guiding principle in the solution of this problem is that when someone is hurt a remedy should be sought to make that person feel better. Therefore, she first gets Tommy's attention back to the conversation by calling him back.

TEACHER:  Tommy, uh-uh, Tommy, Tommy, Tommy! [*In the meantime, she encourages Mark to express his feelings.*]

TEACHER:  [*To Mark*] Tell him how that makes you feel.

MARK:  It makes me feel sad. [*Tommy continues to ignore Mark until the teacher intervenes.*]

TEACHER:  Uh-uh, stop playing. Do you hear him? Turn around. He's talking with you.

MARK:  [*As soon as he feels he has Tommy's attention he expresses his feeling to Tommy.*] It made me feel bad.

In the next section, we will illustrate that as soon as Tommy hears Mark, the teacher builds on Mark's expression of his feelings to lead the children to bring the conflict to a solution.

A second common way in which a teacher assists children to talk about the affect of conflict involves asking children to identify with the feelings of the peers with whom they had the conflict. A typical conflict that may warrant this practice involves hurt, especially hurt without justification. In her effort to help the children in such a conflict to understand that acts leading to hurt are not acceptable, the teacher may ask the children to express how they would have felt if they were the hurt child. The following conversation illustrates how a teacher guides children to identify with their peer, to indicate to the group that isolating a peer hurts.

The four girls who have been playing with Sally in the sand area leave her alone due to a conflict over the use of toys, and they move toward the kitchen area in the classroom. One of the girls complains to the teacher, "She's fighting with us," apparently to justify their act. In turn, the teacher tries to help them understand how their action may have affected Sally by asking them to identify themselves with Sally.

TEACHER:  What if someone told you they don't wanna play with you and
    everybody else was playing? Your feelings would be hurt, wouldn't they?
GIRLS:  Yes.
TEACHER:  You'd be angry?
GIRLS:  Yes.
TEACHER:  You'd be sad?
GIRLS:  Yes.
TEACHER:  OK, then don't do to other people like that; treat people the way you
    want them to treat you, OK? So can she play?
GIRLS  [*All nod their heads*].
TEACHER:  You can go play in the sand.
ONE OF THE GIRLS:  [*To Sally*] You wanna jump rope with us?

As this interaction illustrates, questioning children about their feelings
and providing the value necessary to solve the problem may enable children
to work toward understanding one another.

**Working Toward a Solution.**  For us, the important educational goal is
to help children understand that interpersonal conflict is a problem that
requires a solution. Therefore, presenting to children the need to work toward
resolving a conflict is as important as helping children to solve a given conflict.
A given conflict may not be resolved for many reasons. For example, sometimes children lose interest even after they request teacher assistance. Sometimes the teacher may ask children to think further about their conflict on their
own, leaving the resolution open, especially when she thinks that the children
have not yet made enough effort to resolve it by themselves.

However, when the children and the teacher agree to resolve the children's
conflicts, the teacher should make the guiding cultural value available for children to use in solving the problem. For example, in the case of Tommy and
Mark, the teacher continues to remind children that something should be done
to help a hurt child. Also, the teacher continues to structure the conversation
by her explicit questions, which lead the children to discover a mutually
acceptable solution to their conflict.

Right after Mark declares that he feels bad, the teacher guides the interaction as follows:

TEACHER:  So, what do you think, Tommy? What do you think we can do? He
    feels sad 'cause he's—
TOMMY:  I don't know.
TEACHER:  Well, you think there's some way you can make him feel better?
TOMMY  [*Nods*].
TEACHER:  How can you make him feel better?
TOMMY  [*Takes something, what may be pretend money, from the table and hands it
    to Mark*].
TEACHER:  [*To Mark*]  What do you want him to do to make you feel better?
MARK:  Say he's sorry.

TOMMY:  I'm sorry.
TEACHER:  [*To Mark*]  Is that all right by you?
MARK  [*Nods his head*].
TEACHER:  [*To Mark*]  Did you wanna play with this? [*Points to what Tommy gave him.*]
MARK  [*Nods*].

In this case, teacher assistance offered in the form of guiding questions reached its goal of enabling children to communicate about their conflict. Mark's hurt was the first dimension of the conflict addressed among these children. However, acknowledging Mark's hurt and remedying it brought the entire conflict to a resolution.

## Conclusion

We have presented a practice of how teachers assist preschoolers in their conflict resolution in an urban and inner-city community. Our illustrations indicate that in this community teachers' guidance of children toward resolution of their conflicts occurred in two ways. First, the teachers simultaneously structured the children's interactions and assisted them. When the children were willing to work with one another in bringing their conflict to a solution, a teacher could guide children as if she were another peer, without explicitly imposing her adult power on them. This was made possible by asking the children questions about what happened, how they felt about what happened, and how their conflict could be resolved. These questions about the substance of children's conflict indirectly structured children's interaction toward understanding one another or toward perspective taking.

A second way in which teachers guided children involved explicitly imposing power on children's interactions. Especially if the teachers felt that not all parties involved in the conflict were working toward resolution, the teachers structured children's interactions by giving directives about the interaction rather than by asking questions about the substance of the conflict. This form of guidance was illustrated in how the teacher kept Tommy in the interaction when he attempted to avoid it.

We believe that the most effective way to assist children with their conflicts is to guide them with questions toward the acceptable resolution rather than to tell them what to do. Guiding children by questions enables the children to discover the values that regulate interpersonal matters in their culture on the basis of their own experiences. Children may not be able to understand the values when stated in terms of declaratives, or they may not be able to apply them to their own experiences. It remains to be seen in future work, however, what sort of communication with children proves to be beneficial in their appropriation of cultural values in the resolution of their conflicts.

Although the paramount U.S. cultural value of adults described by some scholars is that talking about conflict is undesirable (Valsiner and Cairns,

1992), we feel that engaging in explicit communication with children about conflict resolution is a valued activity. Since schooling of children in the Western world relies heavily on expression of self and use of language, talking with children about their conflict proves to be a consistent practice. In fact, we feel that conflict resolution should be actively instituted as part of the curriculum in the preschool. Children's conflicts emerging from their peer interactions provide a natural opportunity for a teacher to help children construct shared understanding. Also, teachers should develop curricula that foster occurrence of conflicts so that children can find themselves in problematical interpersonal situations, the resolution of which requires perspective taking.

We wish to emphasize, however, that the practice described in this chapter reflects what is valued about children's education and development in a given culture. Although we value cooperative adult-child relationships, we realize that this value may not be recognized in other cultures. It is important to expand in future work the understanding of how children's conflicts are valued by teachers in other cultures, both in the United States and elsewhere, and how teacher assistance with children's conflicts occurs. This kind of work would provide knowledge about how children's conflicts are conceptualized in diverse cultures, and possibly result in cultural exchange leading to improvement of the ongoing practices.

## Note

1. Vygotsky discussed the creation of the zone of proximal development in play, where the activity itself serves as a guide to children. That discussion is beyond the scope of this chapter. The interested reader is referred to Göncü and Becker (1992).

## References

Bryant, B., and Crockenberg, S. "Correlates and Dimensions of Prosocial Behavior: A Study of Female Siblings with Their Mothers." *Child Development,* 1980, *51,* 529–544.

Cole, M. "Cultural Psychology: A Once and Future Discipline?" In J. J. Berman (ed.), *Nebraska Symposium on Motivation.* Vol. 37: *Cross-Cultural Perspectives.* Lincoln: University of Nebraska Press, 1989.

Corsaro, W., and Rizzo, T. "Disputes in the Peer Culture of American and Italian Nursery-School Children." In A. D. Grimshaw (ed.), *Conflict Talk.* New York: Cambridge University Press, 1990.

Derman-Sparks, L., and the ABC Task Force. *Anti-Bias Curriculum: Tools for Empowering Young Children.* Washington, D.C.: National Association for the Education of Young Children, 1989.

DeVries, R., and Göncü, A. "Interpersonal Relations in Four-Year-Old Dyads from Constructivist and Montessori Programs." *Journal of Applied Developmental Psychology,* 1987, *8* (4), 481–501.

DeVries, R., and Zan, B. *Moral Classrooms, Moral Children.* New York: Teachers College Press, 1994.

Garvey, C., and Shantz, C. U. "Conflict Talk: Approaches to Adversarial Discourse." In C. U. Shantz and W. Hartup (eds.), *Conflict in Child and Adolescent Development.* New York: Cambridge University Press, 1992.

Genishi, C., and di Paolo, M. "Learning Through Argument in a Preschool." In L. C. Wilkinson (ed.), *Communicating in the Classroom*. Orlando, Fla.: Academic Press, 1982.

Göncü, A. "Development of Intersubjectivity in the Social Pretend Play of Preschool Children." *Human Development,* 1993, *36,* 185–198.

Göncü, A., and Becker, J. "Some Contributions of a Vygotskyan Approach to Early Education." *International Journal of Cognitive Education and Mediated Learning,* 1992, *2,* 147–153.

Göncü, A., and Rogoff, B. "Children's Categorization with Varying Adult Support." Paper presented at the annual meeting of the American Educational Research Association, Chicago, 1991.

Greenfield, P. M., and Cocking, R. R. (eds.). *Cross-Cultural Roots of Minority Child Development*. Hillsdale, N.J.: Erlbaum, 1994.

Grimshaw, A. D. (ed.). *Conflict Talk*. New York: Cambridge University Press, 1990.

Grusec, J. E., and Goodnow, J. J. "Impact of Parental Discipline Methods on the Child's Internalization of Values: A Reconceptualization of Current Points of View." *Developmental Psychology,* 1994, *30,* 4–19.

Killen, M., and Turiel, E. "Conflict Resolution in Preschool Social Interactions." *Early Education and Development,* 1991, *2,* 240–255.

Laboratory of Comparative Human Cognition. "Culture and Cognitive Development." In P. Mussen (ed.), *Handbook of Child Psychology*. Vol. 1: *History, Theory and Methods*. New York: Wiley, 1983.

Laursen, B., and Hartup, W. W. "The Dynamics of Preschool Children's Conflicts." *Merrill-Palmer Quarterly,* 1989, *35,* 281–297.

Piaget, J. *The Moral Judgment of the Child*. New York: Free Press, 1932.

Rogoff, B. *Apprenticeship in Thinking*. New York: Oxford University Press, 1990.

Rogoff, B., Mistry, J., Göncü, A., and Mosier, C. *Guided Participation in Cultural Activity by Toddlers and Caregivers*. Monographs of the Society for Research in Child Development, no. 236. Chicago: University of Chicago Press, 1993.

Rommetveit, R. "On the Architecture of Intersubjectivity." In R. Rommetveit and R. M. Blakar (eds.), *Studies of Language, Thought, and Verbal Communication*. Orlando, Fla.: Academic Press, 1979.

Ross, H., and Conant, C. "The Social Structure of Early Conflict: Interaction, Relationships, and Alliances." In C. U. Shantz and W. Hartup (eds.), *Conflict in Child and Adolescent Development*. New York: Cambridge University Press, 1992.

Selman, R., Schorin, M., Stone, C., and Phelps, E. "A Naturalistic Study of Children's Social Understanding." *Developmental Psychology,* 1983, *19,* 82–102.

Shantz, C. U. "Conflicts Between Children." *Child Development,* 1987, *58,* 283–305.

Shantz, C. U., and Hartup, W. (eds.). *Conflict in Child and Adolescent Development*. New York: Cambridge University Press, 1992.

Shweder, R. "Cultural Psychology: What Is It?" In J. W. Stigler, R. A. Shweder, and G. Herdt (eds.), *Cultural Psychology: Essays on Comparative Human Development*. New York: Cambridge University Press, 1990.

Trevarthen, C. "Communication and Cooperation in Early Infancy: A Description of Primary Intersubjectivity." In M. Bullowa (ed.), *Before Speech: The Beginning of Human Communication*. New York: Cambridge University Press, 1979.

Trevarthen, C. "Universal Cooperative Motives: How Infants Begin to Know the Language and Culture of Their Parents." In G. Jahoda and I. M. Lewis (eds.), *Acquiring Culture: Cross-Cultural Studies in Child Development*. London: Croom Helm, 1988.

Tudge, J., Lee, S., and Putnam, S. "Young Children's Play in Socio-Cultural Context: Examples from South Korea and North America." Paper presented at a symposium, "The Pretend Play Cultures: Cultures of Pretend Play," A. Göncü and A. Nicolopoulou, chairs, at the biennial meeting of the Society for Research in Child Development, Indianapolis, Ind., March 1995.

Valsiner, J., and Cairns, R. "Theoretical Perspectives on Conflict Development." In C. U. Shantz and W. Hartup (eds.), *Conflict in Child and Adolescent Development.* New York: Cambridge University Press, 1992.

Vygotsky, L. S. *Mind in Society: The Development of Higher Mental Processes.* Cambridge, Mass.: Harvard University Press, 1978.

Wertsch, J. "The Zone of Proximal Development: Some Conceptual Issues." In B. Rogoff and J. V. Wertsch (eds.), *Children's Learning in the "Zone of Proximal Development."* San Francisco: Jossey-Bass, 1984.

Wertsch, J. (ed.). *Culture, Communication, and Cognition.* Cambridge, Mass.: Harvard University Press, 1985a.

Wertsch, J. *Vygotsky and the Social Formation of Mind.* Cambridge, Mass.: Harvard University Press, 1985b.

*ARTIN GÖNCÜ is associate professor in the Department of Educational Psychology and coordinator of the graduate program in early childhood education at the University of Illinois at Chicago.*

*VIRGINIA CANNELLA is an early childhood educator in an Illinois state prekindergarten program.*

*Three models of family intervention process frame this investigation of children's autonomy and parents' authority in the resolution of sibling conflicts. These issues are explored with observations of parents' interventions in 2,400 sibling disputes between children aged two, four, and six.*

# Autonomy and Authority in the Resolution of Sibling Disputes

## Hildy Ross, Jacqueline Martin, Michal Perlman, Melissa Smith, Elizabeth Blackmore, Jodie Hunter

Sibling conflict is a fairly routine, even commonplace interaction in most families with young children. Disputes may occur over property, the progress of play, or the harm children do to one another. As issues arise, parents often find themselves at the center of their children's disputes. Our research over the past eight years has focused on observations of conflicts between young siblings, how parents become involved in these encounters, what they do to try to help the children settle their differences, and what children might learn about family life from the interventions of their parents.

Developmental psychology provides three important models that we have applied to our examinations of parents' roles in their children's conflicts. First, there is Piaget's well-known position (1932) that parents actually impede their children's understanding of morality, which develops instead through interaction with agemates. According to Piaget, mutual respect between equals enables children to comprehend that justice based on reciprocity is essential to preserving cooperative relationships. In contrast, parents endorse contradictory rules that are not well understood by their children. More important, because these rules derive their force from the parent's authority and are thus external to the child, they are antithetical to a morality based on the free and mutual acceptance of moral principles. According to Piaget: "Resting as it does on equality and reciprocity, justice can only come into being by free consent.

Our research was supported by grants from the Social Sciences and Humanities Research Council of Canada. We are grateful to the families who participated in the study and to those who assisted in collecting and transcribing the data.

Adult authority, even if it acts in conformity with justice, has therefore the effect of weakening what constitutes the essence of justice" (1932, p. 319). In fact, Piaget described parents as taking pleasure in making their children acquiesce to the parents' wills. For these reasons, many followers of Piaget have suggested that adults should refrain from intervention in children's conflicts. At the same time, Piaget did allow for the possibility of some parental contribution to children's understanding of morality. Parents may instill a sense of justice in their children only to the extent that they operate on the premise of their own equality with their children and allow children autonomy in resolving moral issues. Piaget did not expect, however, that parents would often follow these precepts.

Research and thinking about processes of moral socialization and internalization provide a second relevant theoretical model. From this perspective, we consider children's conflict actions as transgressions of the rights and welfare of their siblings (Grusec and Goodnow, 1994; Hoffman, 1979). If children are aggressive, through either physical actions or unkind words; if they take toys without permission or refuse to share; if they interfere with private activity, damage their siblings' property, boss, tease, or threaten one another, then they are violating the moral standards of family life. Parents' responsibilities in such situations might be to interrupt the problematic actions, clarify the family's interpersonal moral rules, explain why they are important, and point out the ways in which each child's actions transgress these standards and harm the sibling. Parents would thereby take positions on the issues that divide the children and enforce the standards that the parents endorse. Moreover, the socialization process need not be totally unidirectional; it could also encompass active contributions from the children. Negotiation might take place as children justify their own actions, explain circumstances that their parents may have overlooked, and even convince their parents with their arguments (Kuczynski, Kochanska, Radke-Yarrow, and Girnius-Brown, 1987; Perlman and Ross, in press). Indeed, it is authoritative parents who are depicted as being particularly attentive to their children's perspectives (Baumrind, 1971). Nevertheless, the outcomes of children's disputes should generally exemplify and contribute to the family's development and the children's internalization of moral standards for interpersonal conduct.

A third perspective on parents' interventions places them in the role of third parties to the conflicts of their children. This perspective begins with the premise that children's actions are part of a conflict rather than a series of moral transgressions (Shantz and Hartup, 1992). Conflict is defined by the relationship of opposition wherein antagonists hold incompatible positions. If parents participate in their children's disputes, they do so as third parties, and the form of their interventions can be examined in relation to the varied means by which third parties influence the conduct and outcome of disputes (Black, 1993; Pruitt and Carnevale, 1993). One dominant distinction in that literature relates to whether the third party has and exerts the power to make and enforce independent decisions concerning the resolution of the conflict. Alternatively, a third party could act to facilitate processes whereby antagonists arrive at mutually satisfactory resolutions of their own issues. A parent who is consistently biased in support of one of his or her children might be considered a partisan third party; a parent who listens to what the children have to say and then decides how the issue should be resolved is an arbitrator; a parent who facilitates processes of resolution between his or her children without forcing a solution on them could be viewed as a conflict mediator.

Thus the moral constructionist perspective cautions parents to stay out of the conflicts of their children or to grant children full autonomy in the mutual resolution of issues even when the children themselves are antagonists. The moral socialization perspective suggests that parents should enforce moral standards that are appropriate for family life, and that parents should be consistent, provide clear rationales for their rules, and consider the alternative viewpoints that their children express. The focus on child conflict emphasizes that the parental role is that of a third party to their children's disputes. Distinctions among third-party roles focus rather directly on the exercise of power with respect to the relationships of others, and can be applied even when the third parties are parents and the "others" in question are their own children. In previous analyses, we have moved among these three perspectives, attempting to illuminate parents' and children's contributions to the intervention process. To create the context for this chapter, we will review some of the general findings from our quantitative analyses of parents' interventions in the disputes of their offspring. However, the theme of this volume inspired a renewed examination of our data. The question we now ask is whether adults can intervene in the conflicts they observe between young children and at the same time foster a sense of autonomy and independence in the children's interpersonal problem solving. In the second half of this chapter, we detail a more qualitative analysis of the tenor of parents' interventions and children's interaction. We ask what presumptions parents and children make with respect to the balance of parental authority and child autonomy in the context of interpersonal disputes. To what extent and how do parents' interventions or children's interactions convey either that parents have the authority to determine the way in which conflicts will be settled between siblings or, alternatively, that children have the autonomy, ability, and responsibility for finding mutually satisfactory resolutions to their own disputes? From the moral constructivist and the socialization perspectives, this question relates to whether parents must always act as authorities who thereby deprive their children of the experience of establishing moral rules based on reciprocity, or whether authoritative parents can foster this process. From the child conflict perspective, this is a question of whether parents can and do act as true mediators of their children's disputes, helping the children to communicate and negotiate but leaving the ultimate decision-making power in the hands of the children.

## Parental Interventions in Children's Conflicts

In recent years, we have explored questions about the prevalence and form of parents' intervention in their children's disputes and about the kind of conflict issues parents are most likely to address. We have emphasized parental enforcement of interpersonal rules for their children's interaction (Ross and others, 1994). In addition, we have focused attention on children's property disputes and on their use of physical aggression (Martin and Ross, 1995; Ross, 1996). We have isolated children's tattling for intensive analysis (Den Bak and Ross, in press), and examined conflicts in which the positions that parents endorse are not realized when conflicts are resolved (Perlman and Ross, in press). We have established that mitigating circumstances influence family reactions to children's transgressions (Martin and Ross, in press). All of these analyses are based on our longitudinal observations of forty families with children who were two and four years of age at our first observation period, and four and six years at our second. When we first observed them, all of the families had two children who were the focus of our observations. Two years later one family had moved away, ten families had an additional child, and in four families the parents were divorced or in the process of separating.

Our observations were conducted in the families' homes and generally consisted of six ninety-minute observation sessions in each observation period. An observer described family interaction and directly recorded on audiotape what family members said. For observation sessions to proceed, children were required to be together, and parents were required to be nearby so that they would be aware of their children's interactions. For half of the observations, all family members were present, and for the other half, mothers and children were observed without the fathers' presence—constellations that were common in these families. Sessions with mothers were increased whenever fathers were not available. For some analyses, we have been able to separate mothers' and fathers' reactions (Lollis, Ross, and Leroux, in press). For other analyses, where we have examined processes that occurred less frequently, we have grouped together both types of sessions and the responses of both parents to create an overall picture of the information that children received from both parents. The data described hereafter are all based on averages for each family during the total of nine hours of observation in each period.

**How Often Do Siblings Fight?** In nine hours of observation, we found conflicts in every family, and a substantial number of conflicts in most families. In the first observation period, families experienced fifty sibling conflicts, and in the second period, there were thirty-six; this is a clear and significant decline, although it is also apparent that the children continued to fight with one another in the second period. At both times, older siblings initiated approximately 60 percent of the conflicts. We also examined the content of the conflicts, by looking both at issues of contention and at the violations of potential family rules by each child, which were coded in parallel. For example, the issue might be coded as physical aggression, and each sibling's aggressive actions would be counted as violations of a rule that prohibits physical aggression. Within a single conflict, there could be one or several conflict issues, and as each conflict issue unfolded, there could be one or several violations by either or both of the children. In the first period, there were 108 issues and 173 violations within 58 conflicts on average; in the second period, there were 89 issues and 150 violations within 36 conflicts. Thus as the number of conflicts decreased their complexity increased in that the average conflict contained 1.8 issues during the first period and 2.5 issues during the second period; during both periods, an average of 1.6 violations occurred in relation to each issue.

**How Often Do Parents Intervene?**  Parents did become involved in a substantial number of their children's conflicts; in 60 percent of disputes between two- and four-year-olds and in 63 percent of disputes between four- and six-year-olds, there was some form of parental participation. The average number of parental interventions in each conflict was 2.3 during the first period and 2.6 during the second. Thus parents did not grant greater autonomy to older sibling pairs than to younger ones, if we measure autonomy in terms of parents' involvement in their children's conflicts. Because conflicts were more complex in the second period, it is also possible to consider less frequent parental involvement in the resolution of each issue within a conflict as an indication of the children's autonomy. Here, too, we did not find a substantial decline in parental involvement across time, with parental intervention occurring with respect to 51 percent of the issues contended by children in the first period and 47 percent of the issues between the same children two years later.

A third metric of parental involvement relates parental intervention directly to the transgression of family rules by each of the two children. Parents intervened after fewer than half of their children's transgressions, and this rate declined significantly between the first and second years of observation (49 percent during the first period and 41 percent during the second). However, parents' rate of intervention did not depend on whether it was their older or their younger children who transgressed the rights or welfare of their siblings; over the two years, parents intervened following 46 percent of the transgressions of their older children and after 43 percent of the transgressions of their younger children. Thus parents neither granted greater autonomy to older children nor intervened more often to protect younger ones.

We do not know which intervention metric has the greater psychological reality for family members in relation to the children's autonomy. Children may have gotten away with proportionally more transgressions during the second period, but just as many of their conflict issues received parental attention, and the parents still participated in the majority of their conflicts. It is also interesting that because children fight less often when they are older, in the second period there were both fewer interventions and fewer conflicts that they resolved on their own.

**How Do Parental Interventions Relate to Children's Conflicts?**  It was also possible for us to examine the relationship between the structure of the children's disputes and the structure and messages of the parents' interventions. Do parents take account of their children's culpability when they intervene and reprimand transgressors? Or do parents adopt the role of a mediator who works with both antagonists to reach a resolution that is acceptable to both of them? We looked at each parental intervention that was relevant to the children's conflict issues and determined who had been the violator whose actions prompted the intervention, whom parents had addressed when they intervened, and whom parents had supported with their interventions.

These comparisons indicated minimal evidence for parental mediation. Most often, parents addressed the perpetrators and supported the victims of each of their children's transgressions. This pattern held in both years and regardless of which child was the violator or the victim; the proportion of interventions directed to the violator and supporting the victim ranged from .59 to .68 (see Table 5.1). There was a tendency for parents to be more supportive of their younger than their older children in the first time period (.68 versus .61), but this tendency did not appear at all two years later (.59 versus .63). The other pattern in the data was for parents to address the victim and support the transgressor (proportions range from .19 to .28). What parents did not often do, however, was offer their support directly to either victims or perpetrators of sibling transgressions (proportions of .06 to .08 for supporting violators and .05 to .07 for directly supporting victims). Thus parents' interventions nearly always were critical of the children to whom they addressed their remarks.

Overall, parents appropriately took account of the children's culpability in the majority of their interventions. The parents' focus on the perpetrators seems most compatible with their disciplinary roles as conceptualized within models of moral socialization. In the interventions, parents addressed and corrected the child who had wronged his or her sibling, thereby instructing both of their children in the application of moral principles to interpersonal behavior. Conversely, parents did address victims and support transgressors in a substantial minority of their interventions. Were they then confused and inconsistent, as

**Table 5.1. Proportions of Parental Interventions That Address and Support the Perpetrator or the Victim of Children's Transgressions**

|  | Transgressor | | | |
|  | First Period | | Second Period | |
|  | Firstborn | Secondborn | Firstborn | Secondborn |
|---|---|---|---|---|
| Address violator |  |  |  |  |
|   Support violator | .07 | .08 | .06 | .08 |
|   Support victim | .68 | .61 | .59 | .63 |
| Address victim |  |  |  |  |
|   Support violator | .19 | .24 | .28 | .24 |
|   Support victim | .07 | .07 | .06 | .05 |

Piaget has suggested, or were they actively mediating, attempting to bring their children into greater harmony by forging compromises between autonomous antagonists? It is important to note that although parents directly addressed one of their children, the other was clearly involved in the conflict and was an indirect recipient of the parents' messages. Indeed, children may be in a better position to appreciate parents' positions on issues when they are either innocent victims or bystanders rather than perpetrators of sibling transgressions. Finally, the fact that parents did not often provide direct support for their children means that children experienced their parents' support indirectly, through the critical comments that parents directed to their siblings. This may create a dynamic within families whereby disciplinary action directed toward one sibling comes to be valued by the other. Indeed, children's tattling to parents may well reflect their desire to highlight their own virtues through the contrast with their siblings' misdeeds (Den Bak and Ross, in press).

**How Do Interventions Influence the Way Conflict Issues Are Resolved?** In addition to supporting one or the other child in their interventions, parents also took positions on conflict issues. Some indication of the parents' authority or the children's autonomy can also come from the relationship between the outcomes of conflicts that children resolved on their own and those that they settled with parental intervention. To what extent do parents' interventions determine the principles by which children's issues are resolved?

We found that parents' impact depended on the particular issues that children disputed. Four conflict issues illustrate these patterns. The first two are disputes concerning entitlement to property: in one the same child both owns and possesses something that the sibling attempts to take; in the second, one child is the owner and the sibling the possessor of disputed property. The third issue involves property damage, and the fourth physical aggression. When parents intervened in the property disputes, they considered both who owned and who currently possessed the property, argued equally for both principles, and supported owners decisively only if the owner also happened to possess the disputed object when the conflict began. Proportions of parental support for owner-possessors averaged .63 and .70 in the first and second observations respectively; and for owners who opposed possessors averaged .56 and .57 (see Table 5.2). In contrast, parents more decisively and consistently enforced rules regarding the other two issues: children should neither damage their siblings' property nor aggress physically against one another (proportions ranged from .77 to .94).

When conflicts ended, the parents' positions were not always realized. When ownership was an issue, children who were owners generally ended up with the objects, regardless of who originally possessed them and whether or not parents had intervened (see Table 5.2). This effect was especially strong when rights of ownership were pitted against those of possession, the very situation in which parents' interventions did not consistently favor either side. Additionally, the children, far more than their parents, made claims of ownership to support

**Table 5.2.  Parental Interventions and the Outcomes of
Children's Disputes**

| Issue | First Period | | | Second Period | | |
| | Parent Supports Rule | Outcomes Uphold Rule | | Parent Supports Rule | Outcomes Uphold Rule | |
| | | With Intervention | Without Intervention | | With Intervention | Without Intervention |
| --- | --- | --- | --- | --- | --- | --- |
| Ownership plus possession | .63 | .71 | .76 | .70 | .63 | .67 |
| Ownership versus possession[a] | .56 | .70 | .74 | .57 | .67 | .82 |
| Property damage | .83 | .73 | .44 | .77 | .85 | .42 |
| Physical aggression | .93 | .71 | .26 | .94 | .71 | .24 |

Note: The data are the proportions of parental interventions that support rather than oppose a given rule, or the proportion of conflict outcomes that uphold rather than contravene a given rule when parents have or have not intervened.

[a] Figures are the proportion of parents supporting and outcomes upholding the rights of owners.

their positions within disputes. Thus children assumed a fair degree of autonomy in determining the resolutions of their property disputes. Even when parents had intervened, families resolved such conflicts in accordance with a principle that was reflected more strongly and consistently in the children's behavior than in the interventions of their parents (Ross, 1996). In contrast, parental authority was exercised more clearly when property was damaged or siblings were assaulted physically. Then outcomes upheld rules that prohibited these transgressions, but only when parents had intervened; otherwise, children showed little regret and seldom offered reparation for the harm they had done, nor did they generally cease their actions in response to requests from their siblings. Moreover, parents were no more influential in this respect during the second observation period than they had been during the first period. Does this mean that the exercise of parental authority undermined the development of equitable moral principles for the resolution of children's conflicts? Did the lack of decisiveness that parents show about property actually foster the development of a consistent justice-based principle upon which the children could depend? These results are certainly compatible with the logic of Piaget's position.

**Autonomy and Authority.**  What have we learned about autonomy and authority from these quantitative analyses? First, it is clear that parents were often involved in their children's conflicts and that this did not change substantially between the young ages we studied. Even if parents had intervened less often, it would be difficult to determine the meaning of the simple fact of intervention versus nonintervention without also looking at the quality of the parents' interventions. If parents consistently exercise their full authority when they do intervene, then their failure to intervene might only indicate that their children's current conflicts do not create enough of a disturbance for the parents to bother, rather than indicating parental granting of autonomy to the chil-

dren. We also found that parents' interventions were largely directed to perpetrators and generally supported the victims of transgressions, which gives a
sense of the generally authoritative style of a disciplinarian. Finally, it was clear
that on some matters parents were quite decisive and enforced their positions
in the conflicts in which they intervened; property damage and physical
aggression exemplified the processes that clearly illustrate the exercise of
parental authority. On other matters, principally those that involved ownership, parents were less decisive and children appeared to develop equitable
principles that were applied regardless of parental intervention. In these cases,
parents might have been acting more as mediators in their children's disputes.
It is also possible, however, that parents still did take an authoritative stance
but that in property disputes they were dealing with issues that were not serious for them and that this fact rather than the sharing of power with their children accounted for the inconsistencies in their interventions. Because of the
questions that remained after these quantitative analyses were completed, we
have looked anew and more directly at the exercise of authority and the granting of autonomy in parental interventions.

## A Qualitative Analysis of Parental and Child Power in Sibling Conflict Resolution

Our procedure was to reexamine collectively the approximately 2,400 conflicts
in which parents had intervened. We sought examples of parents indicating
explicitly or implicitly that the children should resolve issues autonomously
and cases in which the children did so. To counter this evidence, we also
searched for examples of family members indicating that issues should be
resolved through the exercise of parental authority. Throughout this process,
we discussed the conflicts we had selected, challenged one another's interpretations, and categorized our joint sample of events. Where evidence was relatively explicit and rare (such as direct requests by parents for children to
resolve the issue by talking to one another), we collected each example we
found in the data. Where evidence was more frequent and indirect (such as
parents threatening their children), we collected only a sample of the events
for purposes of illustration.

**Parents Invite Their Children's Autonomy.** Parents told their children
to resolve issues on their own in varied ways, but not frequently. Explicit
requests that children work out their problems by themselves or that they
speak directly with their siblings occurred seventeen times. Two examples of
such requests follow, one from each observation period.

### Example from First Period
YOUNGER CHILD:  Mom, Mark not fair.
MOTHER:  Why not?
[*The older child had gathered together some boxes that they were cutting and had
put down only one for his younger brother to use.*]

YOUNGER CHILD:  He gave me one.
MOTHER:  Hmm?
YOUNGER CHILD:  He gave me one already.
MOTHER:  Jason, instead of calling mommy for things like that, I think you should go work it out by yourself, OK?
YOUNGER CHILD:  OK.
MOTHER:  And if you can't work it out by yourself, then you call me, but try it by yourself first.

### Example from Second Period

OLDER CHILD:  [*To mother*] Sally wants to play with my Ghostbuster's car.
MOTHER:  Can't she play with your car?
OLDER CHILD:  No.
MOTHER:  Why?
OLDER CHILD:  I don't want her to.
MOTHER:  Well, then, you tell her then.
OLDER CHILD:  Pardon?
MOTHER:  If you don't want her to play, then you tell her that.
OLDER CHILD:  What?
MOTHER:  I said, if you do not want her to play with something of yours, you tell her that, but don't tell me to tell her.

Given that children did not often hear this message from their parents, it is not surprising that the child in the second example twice asked his mother to repeat herself; this was the only time in our observations that he was asked to deal directly with his sibling.

We found about a dozen examples in which parents either referred decisions about issues to one of the children or conveyed one child's authority to the sibling, as illustrated in the following examples:

### Example from First Period

OLDER CHILD:  [*To mother*] You don't eat my grapes without asking—you say that to him, OK?
MOTHER:  [*To younger child*] Ian told me to tell you, "Don't eat his grapes without asking."
YOUNGER CHILD:  [*To mother*] Yucky grapes!
OLDER CHILD:  [*To younger child*] They weren't yucky!

The mother in this real-life sour grapes story spoke not on her own authority but explicitly with the authority of the child who owned the grapes in question. The authority to resolve this issue thus remained with the children. In a second example, a boy sought his mother's permission, but she referred the issue to her daughter and later reinforced her daughter's decision. When the brother directly addressed his sister, she consented to his request.

### Example from First Period

OLDER CHILD: [*To mother*] Can I do that for Becky [*color part of the picture she's doing*]?

MOTHER: [*To younger child*] Can Ben do yours, Becky?

YOUNGER CHILD: [*To mother, fussily*] No.

OLDER CHILD: [*To younger child*] I can. I can do that. I can.

YOUNGER CHILD: [*To older child*] No! No!

MOTHER: [*To older child*] Don't touch it! Don't touch it!

OLDER CHILD: [*To younger child*] I can do it for you, Becky.

YOUNGER CHILD: [*To older child*] OK.

Finally, there were approximately twenty-five conflicts in which parents attempted to increase the success of their children's negotiations, either by coaching those who were trying to gain something from a sibling or by attempting to increase the likelihood that one child's request would be successful if the parents approached the other child themselves. In the following example, a mother used both strategies: after asking her younger daughter to direct her requests to her older sister, she addressed the older child herself in order to increase the chance that the younger child's request would succeed. The mother's reinforcing request, like some of our earlier examples, referred the decision on this issue to her daughter. Next, the mother gave her younger daughter some strategies for dealing with the older child. Finally, she tried again to gain agreement from her older daughter, by minimizing the risk of her refusing. Only then did the older child assent to her sibling's request. Thus, after returning the conflict and the power to resolve it back to her children, this mother attempted to structure her children's interactions to facilitate their reaching a compromise.

### Example from First Period

YOUNGER CHILD: [*To mother*] I want that one [*her sister's coloring book*].

MOTHER: That's Liz's, though, honey.

YOUNGER CHILD: I want Liz's.

MOTHER: You'll have to ask Liz.

YOUNGER CHILD: [*To older child*] I want that book.

MOTHER: [*To older child*] Can she color in your new book? One picture? [*The older child does not reply.*]

MOTHER: [*To younger child*] Ask her, Jodie.

YOUNGER CHILD: [*To older child*] Ya?

MOTHER: [*To younger child*] Just say, "One picture."

YOUNGER CHILD: [*To older child*] One, one. Just do one [*holding up one finger; the older child does not reply*].

MOTHER: [*To older child*] I'll help her. OK? I'll help her so she won't mess your book up. OK?

OLDER CHILD: [*To mother*] OK.

In total, parents intervened and endorsed, encouraged, or insisted on their children's autonomy in sibling conflict resolution in any of the ways outlined in the dialogues just presented (telling children to solve their own problems, deferring to the authority of one of the children, coaching the children's resolution of disputes, or some combination of these methods) in fewer than fifty conflicts. That amounts to 2 percent of the 2,400 conflicts in which parents intervened. Moreover, these instances did not increase from the first to the second observation period, but they were roughly proportional to the incidence of conflict and conflict intervention during each period. Conversely, these instances came from twenty-one different families. Thus parents in approximately half of the families did invite the children's autonomy in at least one conflict, indicating that the notion of children's autonomy was fairly widespread, despite the rarity with which it was realized in parents' interventions. Finally, the examples that we did find clearly illustrate the potential and varied means by which parents could encourage independent problem solving between their children.

**Interventions Based on Parents' Authority.** In the vast majority of interventions, parental authority was assumed and exercised with varying degrees of power. That is, parents might issue unequivocal commands ("You're not getting the markers"), make weaker requests or suggestions that sometimes sought their children's agreement ("Why don't one of you have one truck and one of you have the other part. . . . You have to share these. OK?"), use reason ("You think it's OK to hit her?"), or question their children to better decide on an appropriate resolution (Father: "And what did you do?" Child: "Nothing." Father: "You did nothing at all? Are you sure?"). This variety existed throughout the data, and we have not yet directly examined the extent to which parents equivocated or reasoned or directly expressed their authority as they intervened. However, we emphasize three rather clear ways in which parents indicated their authority over their children's conflicts. The first way occurred when parents explicitly told their children to inform them rather than try to resolve the issue directly with their siblings. This way of indicating authority occurred fewer than ten times in the data set. In the following example, a mother instructed her daughter to stay out of the sibling conflict, despite the daughter's reasoned argument in support of her own and the mother's position. This contrasts with the requests of other parents that their children deal directly with one another.

### Example from Second Period

MOTHER: [*To younger child*] Who just tried to play with it?

YOUNGER CHILD: [*To mother, whining*] Amanda. I don't want her to play with it.

OLDER CHILD: [*To younger child*] I let you play with my new set, and, and, you let me—.

MOTHER: [*To older child*] Just a second, Amanda. I'm dealing with it. OK? Can you wait a sec?

YOUNGER CHILD: [*To mother*] It's 'cause I got pinched by it.

[*The conflict continues without the older child's involvement.*]

In the next transcription, the mother also expresses her desire to deal with the children's problem. In addition, the dialogue exemplifies the second explicit means by which parents emphasized their own authority: by citing their word as the basis for moral action. Parents referred in this way to the authority of their prior orders fewer than ten times in our observations.

### Example from First Period

OLDER CHILD:  [*To younger child*] Give it back [*a doll; the younger child fusses*].

OLDER CHILD:  [*To mother*] Mommy. Get my Gem back [*tugs on the doll, which the younger child releases, fussing*].

MOTHER:  [*To older child*] Hey, hey, hey! What have you been told? What have you been told, Katie? That when your sister takes the toy you don't do any of that nonsense. You come to me. I was just getting off the telephone. I was going to get the doll away, but you had to push it. You know better than to do that. You've been told time and time again.

A third statement of parental authority is both less explicit and more frequent in our observations. It involves the use of threats, particularly those in which parents threaten consequences in an unrelated domain. The generality of parents' authority is thereby stressed. Such instances were fairly numerous in our data, and one is cited here for purposes of illustration. Both parents threatened to send a child to his room if he refused to apologize to his sibling for his aggression.

### Example from First Period

FATHER:  [*To younger child*] Alex, you are not supposed to bite Corey. What did you bite him for, huh? [*The younger child does not reply.*] You go and tell him you're sorry. OK? [*The younger child still does not respond.*] C'mon. You go tell Corey you're sorry. Or do you want to go upstairs?

YOUNGER CHILD:  [*To father*] No.

MOTHER:  [*To younger child*] Do you want to go up to your room? [*Younger child does not reply.*]

Thus, in addition to fostering their children's autonomy, parents also expressed rather directly the means by which they wield their own authority in the context of sibling conflicts. More often, however, parental authority was exercised without children also being told to stay out of the dispute, reminded of what the parent has told them before, or threatened. By simply exercising their authority in their children's disputes, parents convey the message that they have authority to exercise. We turn next to the question of whether children accept or challenge their parents' authority over their own disputes.

**Children's Challenges to their Parents' Authority.** There were only six cases in which the children clearly expressed, either to their parents or to their siblings, their desire to solve their own problems independently of parental authority. We cite two of these cases here because they differ greatly in tone. (An additional example also appears in the final example in this chapter.) In the first example, the older sibling told her mother not to intervene, despite the mother's assurance of support for her daughter. In the second example, both children ignored and defied their mother in a conflict they wished to keep between themselves. Despite their competition, they appeared to enjoy the scatological insults they hurled at one another, and resisted their mother's attempts to control their insulting language.

### Example from First Period

OLDER CHILD: [*To mother*] He's not letting me copy on it.
MOTHER:  I know. I'll take care of it when I get off [the telephone].
OLDER CHILD:  No you won't.
MOTHER:  Yes, I will.
OLDER CHILD: [*To mother*] I don't want you to.

### Example from Second Period

OLDER CHILD: [*To younger child*] David is a twerp head.
YOUNGER CHILD:  Jonathan is a twerp head.
OLDER CHILD:  So are you.
YOUNGER CHILD:  Well, you are a poopy bum.
MOTHER: [*To younger child*] That's not nice.
OLDER CHILD:  I'm not talking to you. I'm talking to a different . . . David.
YOUNGER CHILD: [*To older child*] You are a poopy bum. You are a poopy bum.
MOTHER: [*To younger child*] David, David.
OLDER CHILD: [*To younger child*] Who are you saying that to?
YOUNGER CHILD:  Never mind.
MOTHER: [*To younger child*] You never mind saying that please.
YOUNGER CHILD:  You never mind talking.
OLDER CHILD: [*To mother*]:  He can say whatever he wants.
MOTHER:  Not here he can't.
OLDER CHILD:  Yes, he can.
MOTHER:  Well, within reason.

We also noted several other instances in which a child failed to bring a parent into a conflict, notwithstanding our observation that the sibling had deliberately hurt the child. These are less explicit rejections of the parents' involvement than the earlier ones. In the following observation, a two-and-a-half-year-old did not report his sibling's aggression despite the parents' questioning and likely support. Given that these young children frequently tattled to their parents when their siblings were aggressive (Den Bak and Ross, in press), it is plausible that this child lied to keep his parents from intervening.

### Example from Second Period

[*The older child hits the younger child, who begins to cry. The older sibling leaves the room.*]

FATHER: What's the matter?
YOUNGER CHILD: I hurt my back.
FATHER: What happened? Come here.
YOUNGER CHILD: I hurt my back.
MOTHER: Be careful.
FATHER: Oh, your back. Are you OK?

Aside from these specific examples, we also have evidence that individual disputes were not always resolved in the way that parents might have preferred, even when parents did intervene. That is, parents intervened and took positions on issues of dispute, but resolutions were not consonant with the positions the parents had endorsed (Perlman and Ross, in press). This discordance gives evidence of the children's powerful role in resolving disputes even when parents had intervened. Outcomes that were discordant with parents' positions occurred during the first period in 29 percent of the disputes in which parents intervened and during the second period in 16 percent of such conflicts. Thus, across time, parental authority is a more rather than a less potent determinant of conflict resolutions. Because the vast majority of these disputes were not marked by explicit indications by either parents or children that children should be responsible for resolving their own disputes, these conflicts might more appropriately be conceptualized as occasions when children argued, defied, and opposed parents and held their ground until parents either stopped insisting on or actually changed their positions. These disputes provide evidence that parental authority is not all-powerful, but they do not provide evidence of the children's positive responsibilities for resolving their own disputes.

An example follows in which a mother changed her mind in the face of the children's arguments and refusals. Note, however, that the mother spoke with authority in her interventions, even threatening the children several times, but the children did not accept her suggestions for resolution. The children did not resolve the issue on their own; indeed, once their mother had intervened, they directed all of their arguments toward her rather than toward one another.

### Example from First Period
MOTHER: Give the necklace back to your older sister
YOUNGER CHILD: I want to play with it.
MOTHER: No! [*The older child is fussing. To older child.*] Stop that right now.
OLDER CHILD: I had it first.
MOTHER: You didn't have it first.
YOUNGER CHILD: It's mine.
MOTHER: [*To older child*] You did not have it first. Your sister had it first and she gave it to you to play with and you gave her your Gem's stand. [*To younger child.*] Give the necklace back to her.
YOUNGER CHILD: No. I need to play with it.

MOTHER:  [*To both children*] I guess I'm gonna have to take the necklace now, aren't I?

YOUNGER CHILD:  No. [*Older child picks up the Gem stand.*]

MOTHER:  [*To older child*] All right. Your sister plays with the necklace and you play with the doll stand.

OLDER CHILD:  I don't want to.

MOTHER:  Well, fine. Then you'll find yourself in your room.

[*The conflict ends and the older child is not sent to her room.*]

**Children Accept Parental Authority in Their Sibling Conflicts.** Balanced against the children's resistance to their parents' authority are numerous instances of their appealing to parents in the context of conflict, appeals that often took the form of tattling (Den Bak and Ross, in press). Children tattled in the wake of their siblings' transgressions, focusing on issues such as aggression or property damage that were likely to elicit parental support for themselves. Parents hardly ever reprimanded their children for tattling, but they most often intervened in the disputes. We argue that tattling is an indirect appeal for parents to intervene in conflicts, and that children both recognize and utilize their parents' authority when they tell on siblings. Moreover, tattling did not decrease but rather increased from the first to the second observation period (12.7 versus 18.3 times on average within each family), and at both times, older children were more likely to tattle than their younger siblings (18.0 versus 13.0 times, summed over both periods). Thus children used their parents more rather than less often as they developed. In the example that follows, one sister tattled repeatedly until her father finally believed her report. Once that happened, the tattler excused her sister's aggression and they resumed their game.

### Example from First Period

OLDER CHILD:  [*To mother*] Heather bite me.

MOTHER:  [*To younger child*] No biting. [*To older child.*] I think she's just playing.

OLDER CHILD:  [*To father, fussing*] Heather bite me.

FATHER:  Let me see.

OLDER CHILD:  She bite me.

FATHER:  Where? [*Older child holds out arm for father to see.*]

FATHER:  That's no bite on there. [*To younger child.*] Are you biting, Heather? [*Younger child shakes her head no.*]

OLDER CHILD:  Ya, she did! She did!

MOTHER:  [*To younger child*] Heather, OK. You better not bite.

FATHER:  [*To younger child*] No biting. You want me to bite you?

YOUNGER CHILD:  No.

FATHER:  Tell Sarah you're sorry.

OLDER CHILD:  [*To father*] She was playing.

YOUNGER CHILD:  [*To older child*] I'm sorry.

We found only two other cases of children clearly accepting their parents' authority.

### Example from Second Period

YOUNGER CHILD: These are my things.
OLDER CHILD: No. They're mine too.
YOUNGER CHILD: Uh uh.
OLDER CHILD: Mommy's the boss around here, [*To mother*] aren't you?
MOTHER: [*To both*] OK. That's enough.

### Example from First Period

[*The older sibling has just hit the younger, who reciprocates. The older child starts to cry.*]
FATHER: [*To older child*] You had that coming.
MOTHER: [*To older child*] You think it's OK to hit her?
OLDER CHILD: [*To mother*] Uh uh. I better go up for my punishment.
MOTHER: [*To older child*] What do you have to say?
OLDER CHILD: [*To younger child*] I'm sorry.

## Conclusion

Despite the advice of experts, neither parents nor children frequently voiced the idea that children should resolve their own disputes. Parents did make this suggestion more often than their children and used varied and constructive means to support independent conflict resolution. Parents showed us that it would be possible for them to mediate children's conflicts; however, the authority with which they more typically intervened in their children's disputes clearly countered their desire to foster the children's autonomy. While parents did ignore a substantial proportion of their children's disputes, this fact also must be evaluated within the context of the parents' exercise of authority when they did intervene. No dramatic changes occurred in the styles of parental intervention as the children developed. Although the children spoke less often of either autonomy or authority than their parents did, they too generally accepted their parents' authority within their conflicts, and by tattling sought to use that authority to their advantage. As tattling increased with age, it might be that children's acceptance of their parents' authority also increased. This same conclusion follows from the finding that in the first observation period, rather than the second, conflict outcomes were more often discordant with the positions that parents had taken in their interventions.

As third parties to their children's disputes, parents adjudicated far more often than they mediated, reserving for themselves the prerogative of making decisions on their children's conflict issues. In relation to models of socialization, parents' reactions to their children's transgressions ranged from permissive (parents ignored more than half of their children's transgressions, including physically aggressive ones [Martin and Ross, 1995]) to authoritarian (for example, the threats and appeals to the word of the parent mentioned earlier). Conversely, parents also reasoned with their children and listened to reason in their children's arguments (Perlman and Ross, in press). Finally, as Piaget suggested they might, the children did seem to negotiate principles of justice in the property domain that were based on reciprocity and freely accepted; children respected one another's ownership despite the parents' less consistent endorsement of that principle. Thus either children wrested or parents granted some autonomy, not directly or explicitly, and not in all domains of their interaction.

It is clear that our observations speak to patterns that existed within the families that we studied and not to patterns that could possibly emerge if attention were consistently paid to the question of children's autonomy. Half of our parents did show some inclination to mediate, by referring occasional decisions to their children and at the same time facilitating the processes by which their children could come to a fair or generous resolution of a conflict. We would not expect this approach to children's conflicts to be easily adopted by parents of young children; were it the easy route, we might have observed it more frequently. To the extent that conflicts also involve transgressions, parents who fail to take a stance might indicate their acceptance of misbehavior by their children. Consequently, the precise limits to the children's autonomy would have to be drawn and unanticipated, and subtle distinctions would have to be made. Just what constitutes an unacceptable misdeed and what constitutes a means of independent conflict resolution will not be easily conveyed given the complexities of everyday family life. These difficulties are well illustrated in a final conflict example. In the earlier portions of this long dispute, the children took and damaged toys that the other was playing with, as well as insulted, interfered with, excluded, tattled on, hit, and bit one another. The conflict extended beyond the portion included in the example. The older sibling returned to the playroom, found her younger sister playing with her things, hit her over the head, and then retreated in frustration to play with something else. In the portion of the fight that we have excerpted, the mother and her older daughter negotiated the limits of the autonomy that both mother and child endorsed. The negotiation was not limited to reasoned argument, but included commands, threats, and defiance. The child's early appeal to the mother's authority, and the mother's definitive comments on the means of conflict resolution, give some indications that the limits of autonomy were not clearly drawn before the dispute but may have to emerge within the emotional context of family conflict.

### Example from Second Period

YOUNGER CHILD: [*To mother, whining*] Amanda. I don't want her to play with it. [*The younger sister reenters the room after the mother warns her not to wreck her older sister's playthings.*]

OLDER CHILD:  [*To mother*] Mommy, no! [*Appeals to authority. Younger sister steps on older sister's things.*]

OLDER CHILD:  [*To younger child*] Stop! [*Younger child picks up some of older child's toys.*]

MOTHER:  [*To older child*] Sara. Stop yelling.

OLDER CHILD:  But mommy. Keep her away. [*Appeals to authority.*]

MOTHER:  I'm not going to take her away. You have to work at handling it too when she gets in your way. [*Invites autonomy.*]

OLDER CHILD:  I'm trying.

MOTHER:  Trying is not yelling. [*Coaches autonomy.*]

OLDER CHILD:  [*To mother, yelling*] I don't.

MOTHER:  Sara.

OLDER CHILD:  I said stop, when . . . but she won't stop so all I have to do is yell.

MOTHER:  Sara. You have a choice. Sara, you can stop yelling or you can go to your room. [*Threatens.*]

OLDER CHILD:  I don't. [*Defies mother.*]

MOTHER:  All right. Yelling is not a way to deal with it. [*Coaches autonomy but from a position of authority.*]

OLDER CHILD:  Deana should go to her room. I don't like her. She's not my sister anymore.

MOTHER:  Sara.

OLDER CHILD:  I'm not—.

MOTHER:  Yelling doesn't solve anything. [*Coaches autonomy.*]

OLDER CHILD:  She's not [solving anything either].

MOTHER:  You try to talk it out without yelling. [*Coaches autonomy.*]

OLDER CHILD:  Mommy..

MOTHER:  Um hum?

OLDER CHILD:  [*Yells*] It's not your problem so get out of it! [*Demands autonomy.*]

MOTHER:  Sara, it is my problem, as well as yours. [*Asserts authority.*]

OLDER CHILD:  No it isn't. [*Demands autonomy.*]

MOTHER:  You're yelling at me, so. . . . [*Asserts authority.*]

OLDER CHILD:  Yeah, well that's not the same problem me and Deana are on so get off her problem. [*Asserts autonomy.*]

MOTHER:  Sara, would you come here please?

## References

Baumrind, D. "Current Patterns of Parental Authority." *Developmental Psychology Monograph,* 1971, *4* (1), 1–103.

Black, D. *The Social Structure of Right and Wrong.* Orlando, Fla.: Academic Press, 1993.

Den Bak, I., and Ross, H. S. "'I'm Telling!' The Content, Context and Consequences of Children Tattling on Their Siblings." *Social Development,* in press.

Grusec, J. E., and Goodnow, J. J. "Impact of Parental Discipline Methods on the Child's Internalization of Values: A Reconceptualization of Current Points of View." *Developmental Psychology,* 1994, *30,* 4–19.

Hoffman, M. L. "Development of Moral Thought, Feeling, and Behavior." *American Psychologist,* 1979, *34,* 958–966.

Kuczynski, L., Kochanska, G., Radke-Yarrow, M., and Girnius-Brown, O. "A Developmental Interpretation of Young Children's Noncompliance." *Developmental Psychology,* 1987, *23,* 799–806.

Lollis, S. P., Ross, H. S., and Leroux, L. "Family Interaction and the Socialization of Moral Orientation." *Merrill-Palmer Quarterly,* in press.

Martin, J. L., and Ross, H. S. "The Development of Aggression Within Sibling Conflict." *Early Education and Development,* 1995, *6,* 335–358.

Martin, J. L., and Ross, H. S. "Do Mitigating Circumstances Influence Family Reactions to Physical Aggression?" *Child Development,* in press.

Perlman, M., and Ross, H. S. "Who's the Boss? Parents' Failed Attempts to Influence the Outcome of Conflicts Between Their Children." *Journal of Social and Personal Relations,* in press.

Piaget, J. *The Moral Judgment of the Child.* New York: Free Press, 1932.

Pruitt, D. G., and Carnevale, P. J. *Negotiation in Social Conflict.* Pacific Grove, Calif.: Brooks/Cole, 1993.

Ross, H. S. "Negotiating Principles of Entitlement in Sibling Property Disputes." *Developmental Psychology,* 1996, *32,* 90–101.

Ross, H. S., Filyer, R. E., Lollis, S. P., Perlman, M., and Martin, J. "Administering Justice in the Family." *Journal of Family Psychology,* 1994, *8,* 254–273.

Shantz, C. U., and Hartup, W. W. "Conflict and Development: An Introduction." In C. U. Shantz and W. W. Hartup (eds.), *Conflict in Child and Adolescent Development.* New York: Cambridge University Press, 1992.

*HILDY ROSS is professor of psychology at the University of Waterloo, Ontario.*

*JACQUELINE MARTIN is a doctoral student in developmental psychology at the University of Waterloo, Ontario.*

*MICHAL PERLMAN is a doctoral student in developmental psychology at the University of Waterloo, Ontario.*

*MELISSA SMITH is a doctoral student in developmental psychology at the University of Waterloo, Ontario.*

*ELIZABETH BLACKMORE is an undergraduate student in psychology in the Co-operative Education Program at the University of Waterloo, Ontario.*

*JODIE HUNTER is an undergraduate student in mathematics in the Co-operative Education Program at the University of Waterloo, Ontario.*

*This chapter uses Japanese preschool and elementary education as a vantage point to reflect on how children develop the skills to solve conflicts and the will to do so. The distinction between these two contributors to conflict resolution and the practices that facilitate each are explored.*

# Beyond Conflict Resolution Skills: How Do Children Develop the Will to Solve Conflicts at School?

*Catherine C. Lewis*

A teacher at a California elementary school recently complained that her students are "trained in conflict resolution skills but choose not to use them." A principal of a nearby school worried: "Some students abuse the conflict resolution process: they say all the right things in front of me, and then resume fighting as soon as they're out of my sight." Both comments underline the idea that the skills of conflict resolution are not enough—students must also have the will to exercise these skills. Although some U.S. conflict resolution programs attempt to influence students' general cooperative disposition (DeJong, 1994), too often the will is treated as a black box—a victim, perhaps, of American education's general tendency to emphasize discrete skills and behaviors at the expense of broader "dispositions" (Katz, 1993). Throughout this chapter, I use *will* as a synonym for *disposition,* which Katz defines as "the tendency to exhibit frequently, consciously, and voluntarily a pattern of behavior that is directed toward a broad goal" (p. 1).

Japanese education provides an interesting vantage point from which to look at both will and skill as components of conflict resolution. This chapter

Sections of this chapter are based on the author's book *Educating Hearts and Minds: Reflections on Japanese Preschool and Elementary Education* (Cambridge University Press, 1995) and are reproduced by permission of Cambridge University Press. The research reported herein was supported by the Abe Fellowship Program of the Social Science Research Council and the American Council of Learned Societies, with funds provided by the Japan Foundation's Center for Global Partnership, the Nippon Life Insurance Foundation, the Spencer Foundation Small Grants Program, and the Social Science Research Council.

reviews accounts of conflict resolution from Japanese preschools and elementary schools and then explores the idea that although conflict resolution skills may be learned as other skills are learned (for example, through modeling, practice, feedback, and so on), the will to solve conflicts needs to be conceived differently—as a value that is internalized by children, depending in part on characteristics of the school setting. Specifically, schools that meet children's basic psychological needs for autonomy, belonging, and competence—and thereby become valued, important places to children—may foster children's will to solve conflicts (Connell and Wellborn, 1991; Deci and Ryan, 1985; Watson and others, 1989).[1]

## Research Methods

The comments on Japanese preschool and elementary education that follow are based both on my own research (Lewis, 1984, 1988, 1995) and on accounts by other researchers (Cummings, 1980; Easley and Easley, 1983; Kotloff, 1993, 1995; Peak, 1991; Sato, 1991). As Sato's ethnography (1991) reveals, there is considerable variation within Japanese practice; by focusing on general themes, I do not wish to imply that all Japanese schools are uniform in their practice. This chapter focuses on practices (such as use of small groups, cooperative learning, student authority, and shared schoolwide events) that are extremely widespread.

My own observations of Japanese education began seventeen years ago, first with structured two-day observations of fifteen diverse preschools, and then with similar observations of fifteen first-grade classes in the Tokyo public schools. I followed these observations in later years with longer, unstructured observations of up to three months duration in about twenty additional elementary schools in several regions of Japan (see Lewis, 1995, for a fuller description of methods and samples). Though briefer, my observations are remarkably consistent with the independent observations of long-term ethnographers like Nancy Sato (1991) and Lois Peak (1991); they are also consistent with the few systematic cross-national data that are available (Stevenson and Stigler, 1992).

## Japanese Preschools and Elementary Schools: Emphasis on Children's Self-Management

I originally went to Japan expecting Japanese preschool and elementary classrooms to be regimented, adult-controlled settings. For how else could the "indulged" young children described in accounts of Japanese childrearing (Doi, 1973; Vogel, 1963) become the highly disciplined students found in studies of Japan's elementary schools (Stevenson and Stigler, 1992)? My expectation could not have been farther from the mark. At both preschools and elementary schools, teachers kept a remarkably low profile as authority figures. For example, in only 53 percent of spot observations were all preschoolers even within sight of their teacher; elementary students, not teachers, assumed responsibility for many aspects of classroom management, including supervising transitions from recess to study, leading class meetings, and evaluating their own behavior and that of other students (Lewis, 1984, 1995). At the same time that they downplayed their role as authorities, teachers invested heavily in building children's social skills (such as communication and cooperation), their emotional connections to one another and to the teacher, their willingness to buy into classroom practices and values, and their habit of self-critical reflection (Lewis, 1995; see also Easley and Easley, 1983; Kotloff, 1993, 1995; Peak, 1991; Sato, 1991). Before examining why and how Japanese teachers emphasize these qualities, it is worth noting that a number of Western observers have found the emphasis on children's self-management in Japanese schools quite striking. For example, U.S. education researchers Jack Easley and Elizabeth Easley (1983) wrote:

> We noted in Kitamaeno School, as compared with U.S. schools we know, that children are, from the outset, given greater responsibility and treated with greater respect for their own person and their own learning. This is true during and between classes, where, for periods of up to 30 minutes, all the children in the school will be unattended by a teacher or anyone else who is legally responsible for them. . . . When a teacher is absent, other teachers . . . drop in from time to time to assign work to the class, as there are no substitute teachers. . . . A child who disrupts a lesson is rarely singled out for special treatment by the teacher, who usually waits for the disruption to cease or goes on in spite of it. In short, the children are treated more the way we treat adults [pp. 40–41].

The self-discipline of Japanese schoolchildren has, in fact, impressed Western visitors at least as far back as 1919, when progressive educator John Dewey wrote about the Japanese preschools and elementary schools he visited: "They have a great deal of freedom there. . . . The children were under no visible discipline, but were good as well as happy" (Dewey and Dewey, 1920, p. 28).

It is also important to note that despite the eagerness of both Western and Japanese journalists to portray problems ranging from peer bullying to suicide as a regular by-product of the Japanese system, the rates of various antisocial and self-destructive behaviors by Japanese youths remain very low by U.S. standards (see Lewis, 1995, for a review of these data).

In my experience, Japanese teachers talk about conflict resolution both as a matter of skills (noting, for example, that children need to learn to listen to each other and to express themselves) and as a matter of will—or as one Japanese preschool teacher explained it, of developing the "thread between the teacher's heart and the student's heart," the friendships, and the attachment to school that will make children want to solve conflicts and maintain the well-being and harmony of a group they value. The remainder of this chapter explores the techniques that Japanese preschool and elementary teachers use to develop the skills and will of self-management, with the final section speculating on the implications of these techniques for U.S. education.

**Building Social Skills.**  Because Japanese teachers keep a low profile as authority figures, children must solve many problems themselves. A fistfight at a Japanese preschool affiliated with a private university provided the grist for learning skills of conflict resolution (all the names are pseudonyms):

> Two five-year-old boys began to fight over a sand castle, exchanged a few blows, and then became locked in combat, pulling each other's hair and crying, while their preschool teacher looked on. "*Gambare*" ("Do your best"), the teacher cheered on the smaller boy, adding, "Look, Taro's gotten strong; now he can fight without crying." Although the teacher did not intervene herself, she encouraged the children standing nearby to intervene, saying, "Why don't you ask the fighters why they're fighting?" and then, "Tell us what you found out about the fighting," and, "Ask them what would make them stop fighting." After the bystanders described each child's reason for fighting, the teacher responded, "You're the caretakers, so you should decide what to do," and then turned her back on the situation. The "caretakers" encouraged the fighters to apologize to each other, but failed to elicit apologies and gave up. Soon the boys were hitting again, and the teacher asked some other onlookers to intervene. After making this request, the teacher announced, "I am washing my hands of this," and walked away. The onlooker and another girl who had been watching the fight each began to question one fighter, saying, "Why are you fighting?" "Are you still mad? If not, say 'I'm sorry.'"
>
> The teacher, who had been keeping an eye on developments from a short distance away, returned to the fighters and drew a circle in the sand: "Inside this circle are the fighters and the children helping to solve the fight. Everyone outside the circle should begin cleaning up to go home." The two girls who had been questioning the fighters each brushed the sand off one fighter and encouraged him to apologize. After several minutes, the girls finally succeeded in eliciting apologies from both fighters. Each girl held hands with one fighter, and then the girls held hands with each other—forming a chain that linked the fighters. From a distance, the teacher announced, "Great! The problem has been solved, due to Misa and Rie's help." Noticing that one boy was still crying, the teacher said, "Now it's your problem alone, if you've already made up." Although it was already past dismissal time, the teacher discussed the fight with the whole class. She started with a blow-by-blow description, naming the fighters and describing how they had thrown sand, pulled hair, and hit. She also named all four mediators, described their failures and successes in trying to end the fight, and praised them all for helping solve the class's problem. Parents waited for twenty minutes beyond the normal dismissal time while the teacher discussed the fight, described in detail the words and strategies the mediators had used to find out about the fight and elicit apologies, and thanked the mediators by name.

Like the teacher just described, many preschool teachers told me that they allowed some fights to continue (*kenka o mimamoru*) and even that they valued fighting:

When I see kids fighting, I tell them to go where there isn't concrete under them or to go where there are mats. Of course, if they're both completely out of control, I stop it. Fighting means recognizing others exist. Fighting is being equal in a sense.

If children can solve fights on their own without people getting hurt, I let them do it themselves, and ignore it. Kids start out rooting for the weak kid if the teacher stays out of it. If I can, I let them solve it.

If I don't see a fight myself, I get witnesses to tell what happened. Unfortunately, children usually say that the last one to hit is bad. When I'm told about a fight, I get both sides to come, ask both what happened, and get both to agree. I don't try to suppress it, because it will come out somewhere. I also don't listen to tattletales. . . . You have to gain the agreement [*nattoku*] of both sides. For four-year-olds, though, often you can't take the time to do that; you just have to solve fights quickly because there may be fighting somewhere else. With five-year-olds, you have to watch for days afterwards to see how they're treating each other.

The fact that there isn't more fighting among children is considered a problem by many teachers and parents. Teachers plan things so that there will be more fighting—like decreasing the number of toys for five-year-olds. We try to get kids to take responsibility for each other's quarrels. We encourage children to look when someone's crying and to talk about what the child is feeling, thinking, and so forth.

Japanese teachers regarded fighting not so much as a problem between two children as a class problem—and an opportunity. Incidents of fighting, crying, teasing, and other kinds of conflict inevitably resurfaced in teachers' comments at the end of the day. For example, a teacher made the following comments to her class of five-year-olds at the end of a school day at Western Tokyo Preschool:

I'd like to talk about some of the things that happened in our class today. [Describes an incident of sharing she saw.] . . . There was an incident of crying, too. I told you to line up with your friends, and Akiko wanted to line up with some other girls: Mari, Chie, and Emiko. Akiko was crying. And what did you decide to do? [Several girls explain how they decided to hold hands with Akiko, too, because they didn't want her to feel badly.] My heart was very happy to see all this kindness in our class today.

These examples reveal some of the strategies that Japanese teachers commonly use to help children manage conflicts: framing the conflict as the class's problem and encouraging class members to help solve it, teaching children how to elicit each side's perspective and needs, and revisiting the problem with the whole class to build their understanding of what led to the conflict and to its solution. These strategies are generally similar to those employed by conflict resolution programs found in a growing number of U.S. schools (DeJong, 1994). What is strikingly different is the willingness, in some circumstances, to let young children fight. Though not all Japanese teachers agree with this practice, many see it as a way of helping children to develop self-control and learn to intervene in fights before they are old enough to inflict real physical harm on one another. Although Japanese teachers who fail to intervene in fights may help children develop the skills and sense of responsibility needed to act, American educators express concern about the values they are transmitting as they fail to intervene. That force is sometimes acceptable? That it is OK to stand by while someone is hurt? These comments point out the trade-off that educators often face between, on the one hand, making a strong statement of their values, and on the other, allowing children to take personal responsibility and initiative.

That Japanese teachers stood by while children fought did not mean they approved of fighting; the amount of time teachers devoted to class discussion of incidents that occurred and their willingness to give such discussion precedence over other activities (even dismissal) suggests that they regard fighting as a serious problem. Japanese teachers may, however, believe, as an oft-quoted Japanese saying states, that "both parties are to blame in a fight" (*kenka ryoseibai*). If both sides are indeed at fault, then the impetus to intervene on behalf of the "victim" is reduced. In the several fistfights I saw in Japanese preschools, teachers, when they later talked with the class, gave as much emphasis to the provocation (for example, name-calling or exclusion from play) as to the physical aggression itself, with no implication that the person who started hitting was somehow worse than the person who engaged in name-calling. Americans may see a clearer line between verbal and physical aggression.

In addition to learning the skills needed to solve conflicts, Japanese children are expected to learn the skills needed to manage many aspects of classroom daily life—to call the class to order before each lesson, to run class meetings, to clean the classroom and school grounds, and to reflect on how well this has been done. All nineteen first-grade classrooms in which I systematically recorded wall contents had charts designed to help children develop these skills. For example, charts showed the agenda for the brief daily class meetings (for example, "song, greetings, news from classmates, news from teacher") so that students could lead these meetings, as well as the forty-five-minute class meetings that generally occurred once a week. So conflict resolution was but one of many aspects of classroom management for which Japanese children were expected to take responsibility.

**Children's Emotional Connections to Classmates and Teachers.** How do children develop the personal commitment—the will—to solve problems that arise in their interactions with peers? Japanese teachers talk about children's friendships (*tomodachi kankei*), their unity or cohesiveness (*matomari*), and their linking of hearts (*kokoro no tsunagari*) with the teacher and classmates as keys to children's development at school (Lewis, 1995; Shimahara and Sakai, 1992). In their study of on-the-job training for new Japanese elementary teachers, Nobuo Shimahara and Akira Sakai (1992) noted that establishment of *kizuna*—the bond between students and teacher—takes precedence over technical competence; new teachers are urged to "mingle with students without disguise and pretense" (p. 156). They are coached on how to build enduring relationships with children and how to see things from a child's point of view. Here is the kind of advice experienced Japanese teachers gave their new colleagues:

> Teaching is a kind of art. Emphasis should be placed on the relationship of hearts, the nurturing of bonding between the teacher's and children's hearts.
>
> When I get a new class I do not teach subject matter immediately. Instead I play with children intensely for a week to gain a good understanding of them. Then I will begin to know what kinds of children they are and gradually direct them toward the goals of learning on the basis of happy and trustful *kakawari* [personal relations] with them [Shimahara and Sakai, 1992, pp. 156–157].

As one Japanese first-grade teacher put it, "Children don't come to school to learn; they come to school to see their friends." Helping children develop friendships is a central goal of both preschool and elementary education in Japan, emphasized in the national guidelines for each (Monbusho, 1989a, 1989b). At the beginning of the school year, Japanese teachers' magazines are filled with articles on "*gakkyuzukuri*"—promoting a feeling of classroom community. These articles urge teachers to provide chances for students to get to know one another as individuals, to have fun together, and to work together to shape classroom values and practices. I was surprised that none of the nineteen first-grade teachers I interviewed mentioned purely academic skills (such as holding a pencil, writing, or recognizing letters) among the skills and attitudes that children need to learn during the first month of first grade. Two-thirds of the teachers mentioned children's friendships or sense of connection to one another, for example: "At the beginning of the year, I use music to help build our sense of classhood. I use music because I happened to be a music major in college, but you could use any subject—whatever happens to be your favorite. Using music, I give children the opportunity to create something bigger than any one child could create alone. The children share pleasure. They share the satisfaction of creating something together."

Because Japanese elementary students and teachers typically stay together as a unit for two years, they have a long time to create and experience a sense of community. Elementary teachers spend the whole day with their students: students and teacher eat lunch together in the classroom, and the classroom teacher is responsible for all or nearly all subjects, including science, art, music, and physical education. If student work is posted, it is the work of every single student in the class. Likewise, activities that fragment the class—such as pull-out programs and ability grouping—are avoided (Kajita, Shiota, Ishida, and Sugie, 1980; Lewis, 1995).

Teachers help build connections among children through lessons that draw out children's personal experiences and ideas. In many classes, two children each day give one-minute speeches, to tell classmates about their favorite activities outside of school. As part of Japanese language lessons, social studies, and other subject areas, children compose and deliver oral reports on "my most precious possession," share memorable experiences involving their grand-parents, draw each class member's house on a class map, discuss what class members like most and least about school, and find out a great deal about each other's experiences and preferences. Combined with the daily diaries that children in many schools write, these lessons give teachers an amazing array of information about students, which they often use to personalize lessons. Teachers draw individual children into lessons with comments such as "Your grand-mother lives with you, so has she told you about what our neighborhood was like when she was young?" or "Writing is your least favorite subject, so what did you think about today's lesson?" In a society known for "groupism" and uniformity, teachers' interest in personalizing lessons presents an odd paradox. Yet as one teacher pointed out, "To nurture the group, you must nurture each individual." Her comment points out how problematic are the dichotomies, such as individualistic versus collectivistic, often used to describe cultures.

Japanese students also have a chance to get to know one another in the family-like small groups (generally called *han* in elementary schools and *guru-upu* in preschools) that are a prominent feature of life in nearly all Japanese elementary classrooms and in most preschool classrooms. These groups differ sharply from the single-purpose often ability-based groups found in many U.S. elementary schools: they include children with diverse abilities who together pursue a wide range of daily activities from lunch to art projects to chores. Japanese teachers often liken these groups to families and maintain the same groups for a relatively long time: a year or more in preschool and an average of two months in first grade (Kajita, Shiota, Ishida, and Sugie, 1980; Lewis, 1995). Children get to know each other well as they engage in dozens of activities each week within their small groups, and this in fact is one of the goals for the small groups. It is common for the children in each group to talk about the strengths and weaknesses of their cooperation and to reflect on whether they were kind to one another.

Teachers expect the groups to provide a family-like home base for children. As teachers note, "It's hard for children to feel connected to a big class, much easier to feel connected to a group." Many group-building activities give children shared, pleasurable experiences within their groups, such as designing an ideal playground that combines the favorite equipment of each group member, playing games, interviewing each other about hobbies, or performing "paper plays" that combine the drawings made by all group members.

Teachers told me that a good group is "one that works well together," "one that plays well together," and one that has *matomari*. Two descriptions from Tokyo preschools illustrate how teachers use groups to foster children's social skills and connections to one another, and introduce the next theme, children's buy-in to classroom practices and values.

Midway through a morning of free play, Ms. Mikami called together her forty five-year-olds: "Look, everyone can draw a picture that becomes part of a picture drama [*kamishibai*]. Here's how." One at a time she showed five pictures, telling a story that continued across them. She asked children to assemble in their groups. Noise and movement filled the classroom as children roamed and shouted, trying to locate fellow group members. When the five children of each group found one another, they sat down in a circle, put their feet together, lay back on the floor in the shape of a pinwheel, and sat up again. This maneuver left the children of each group facing one another in a circle. "Talk within your group about what kind of a picture drama you want to make. You need to decide what happened and then what happened next, and who's going to draw each part," Ms. Mikami instructed. Over the next thirty minutes, as children planned and drew their pictures, Ms. Mikami circled the room, listening to each group's deliberations. "Will you be able to make a good story if everyone in your group draws the same scene?" she asked the class, after listening to one group's discussion. When she established a listening post outside another group, the students started to tell her what they wanted to make. "It doesn't do any good to tell me. Tell your groupmates what story you want to make," Ms. Mikami said, physically reorienting two girls so that they were facing in toward the group, not outward toward her. Ms. Mikami moved on to listen to another group, where three children were silent and two talked nonstop. "What have you decided?" she asked. When the children replied that they had not yet decided, Ms. Mikami replied, "Then talk about it some more." Once again, only two children talked. Ms. Mikami asked one of the quiet children, "What would you like to draw?" The child described a scene, and Ms. Mikami said to the group: "That's what she's thinking, so listen to her." In the same way, Ms. Mikami encouraged a second quiet child to tell the others what she wanted to draw. Then she engaged the third quiet child: "Everyone's saying this and that, but do you really understand what they mean? If not, you need to ask questions." Finally, the children began to explain to one another what they wanted to draw, and Ms. Mikami went on to observe other groups. The children worked in their groups for about a half-hour altogether, planning, drawing pictures, putting the pictures in sequence, and telling Ms. Mikami their stories. When all groups had finished, Ms. Mikami played a few chords on the piano and announced with a flourish: "It's show time." Students gathered around, and she asked all members of the apple group to raise their hands so that the rest of the class could see who they were. In dramatic tones, she began to tell their story to the class, mentioning the name of each child in turn as his or her drawing was shown. When the story was finished, Ms. Mikami asked the apple group to stand for a round of applause. "Thank you for creating a wonderful picture drama for the class," she said as the apple group members stood, beaming to the class's applause. Ms. Mikami went on to present each group's picture play in the same way, followed by thanks and applause.

At Western Tokyo Preschool, the five-year-old class gathered for the end-of-day meeting. After nearly two hours of freeplay, and a twenty-minute chore time, students seated themselves, each *guruupu* at its own table. "Think about whether you did your chores well," instructed Ms. Shiba. She called on each group in turn, asking members to stand and report to the class on their chores. The children in the first group reported that they had completed their chores; Ms. Shiba thanked them for their hard work. When Ms. Shiba called on the second group, some students were play-fighting and did not hear her. She waited for several minutes, not saying anything, until a classmate nudged the group members to stand. They reported that they had completed their chores, and Ms. Shiba thanked them for their hard work. The third group was similarly slow to stand, and again Ms. Shiba waited quietly without repeating her request. Several members of the group urged the distracted members to stand, and after several minutes they did. "Did you clean the guinea pig cage?" asked Ms. Shiba. "No, we didn't finish," shouted several group members. "Why not?" asked Ms. Shiba. "Because we started playing in the middle," answered one group member. "What can we do if only a few group members are doing a chore, and the rest are off playing?" Ms Shiba asked the class. "The people who get there first should do it all," suggested one class member. "Do you think that's all right?" Ms. Shiba asked, receiving a chorus of protests in response. Another classmate volunteered, "We could get angry at the other people or make them stand in the hall." "Is it a good situation if people work because they are forced to?" asked Ms. Shiba. After several students volunteered their experiences with delinquent choremates, one student suggested, "The people who are working could get together and call the other people in a big voice." Ms. Shiba nodded approvingly at this pragmatic suggestion, repeated it to the class, and called on the next group to report.

**Children's Investment in Classroom Practices and Values.** Ms. Shiba did not upbraid the delinquent guinea pig cage cleaners for their behavior; she did not reward or punish them or tell them what to do next time about the problem. Rather, she elicited suggestions from the children, downplaying their punitive suggestions and highlighting their helpful suggestions. Japanese teachers tend to choose methods of discipline that give children a say in decisions and that deemphasize use of adult authority, surveillance, rewards, or punishment (Lewis, 1984, 1989, 1995; Kotloff, 1993; Peak, 1991). Four strategies for building children's investment in classroom practices are particularly striking. First, all Japanese elementary students—whatever their abilities or personal qualities—regularly serve as leaders. Class monitors (*toban* or *nicchoku*) change daily and have a very visible role as classroom leaders, leading songs, exercises, and lunchtime rituals at preschool, and taking on many additional duties at elementary school, such as leading class discussions, quieting the class, and helping solve problems that arise.

The *toban* system capitalizes on children's natural interests—in attention, prestige, and a chance to lead others—and gives children a chance to experience the pleasure, and headaches, of responsibility. The child standing at the front of the class struggling to quiet classmates could be you—and would be in a matter of days or weeks. As one teacher said, the *toban* system "teaches how hard people can make it for you and how much better it is to have help." As another teacher pointed out, the *toban* system extended the experience of leadership to all children: "The *toban* system allows even a child who can't normally be a leader a chance to be a leader. The children who are least able to lead others in daily encounters are often the ones who work the most carefully when they are *toban*."

Second, students generally help shape the rules and norms of the classroom. At the beginning of the year, students and teacher discuss what kind of class they want to become, and use the results of this discussion to provide the grist for individual, group, and class goals. Usually, the class's major goal is written on a banner over the front blackboard, for example: "Let's be a friendly class that persists until the end," or, "Let's all get along well, cooperate, and do our best." In many classrooms, students talk daily about whether they are making progress toward their goals and what they might do to improve. Children (not teachers) usually suggest some or all of the committees and chore groups that will help the class run smoothly, volunteer for these, carry them out during designated times of the day, and discuss the strengths and weaknesses of their efforts. At brief daily meetings and longer weekly meetings, students often discuss their successes and problems in working toward the kind of class they want to be. Students raise incidents of kindness and exclusion, problems and successes in chores, and ideas for class projects. Typically these meetings are student run.

Third, teachers often keep a low profile as authority figures. One first-grade teacher waited, without saying a word, for seventeen minutes while the student monitors tried unsuccessfully to quiet the class. "I could have quieted them by saying one word, but I don't want to create children who obey just because I'm here," explained this teacher. Later, the class devoted a long class meeting to discussing why they had had trouble quieting down and what they could do to improve. Although teachers' deemphasis on control flies in the face of American conventional wisdom that firm control promotes good behavior, it is quite consistent with attribution theory and research, which suggest that children are most likely to internalize adult values when they see themselves as obeying those values willingly—rather than when they attribute their behavior to external rewards or punishments (Lepper, 1981).

Finally, values—often called the "hidden" curriculum of U.S. schools— are an explicit and ubiquitous part of Japanese elementary education. Students and teachers develop group, class, and school goals; individuals formulate personal goals for their study and life at school; and everyone revisits goals to assess progress. In nineteen first-grade classrooms where I recorded goals intended to be read by children (that is, goals written in phonetic script), there were a total of ninety-four posted goals! Of these, about half focused on friendship, cooperation, and other aspects of social and emotional development: "Let's become friends"; "Let's get along well and put our strength together"; "Let's be kind children who easily say I'm sorry and thank you"; "Let's think about others' feelings before we speak." In other words, skills such as listening were explicitly placed in the larger context of the values they served, such as kindness and consideration.

**Reflection.**   One Japanese first-grade class I studied ended each day by having children think privately about two questions: "Did I do anything kind for others today?" and, "Did I do anything naughty?" Another first-grade class ended the day by discussing progress toward their class goal: "Let's all become friends and put our strength together." Students volunteered examples of kindness (and unkindness) they had witnessed. In yet another class, children ended the day by discussing within their small groups whether their group had met its goal for the week (for example, being "ready to begin each lesson" and working together "in a friendly way").

*Hansei*—reflection—pervaded daily activities (both nonacademic and academic) in the Japanese classrooms I studied. Children reflected in their small groups on whether they had worked together well in doing chores, they identified individual goals for self-improvement and self-assessed their progress on these goals ("to study for one hour every night"; "to raise my hand at least once every day"), and they reflected on their progress toward class goals. *Hansei* was sometimes formal and public. For example, students at one central Tokyo elementary school formally evaluated themselves each Friday on goals chosen by the class, discussing, for example, whether they had made progress toward "becoming a friendly class." In other cases, *hansei* might be private or informal. Students might reflect quietly on their progress in meeting self-identified goals, or they might discuss the day's or week's activities, recalling favorite moments or problems.

Though we currently know little about *hansei,* I think it is an important puzzle piece in our understanding of how children develop the capacity to manage classroom life, including conflicts. The critical inner voice that children develop means that adults have a reduced role as enforcers and can remain benevolent figures. It also means that children are likely to recognize their own contributions to problems and not just the contributions of others— hence the view that both sides are to blame in a fight. In the months that I spent in Japanese elementary schools, I found myself powerfully affected by the reflection going on around me. As students and teachers earnestly asked themselves, "What have I done to help others this week?" and "What are my goals for self-improvement?" I couldn't help asking myself the same questions.

## The Will and Skill of Conflict Resolution in the Classroom

How might the four qualities just described influence children's will and skill in conflict resolution? The contributions to skill are straightforward: as they work together in cooperative groups, run class meetings, handle fistfights, and reflect on their personal contributions to group life, children gain much experience resolving the conflicts that inevitably arise. As we have seen, the needed skills—listening to groupmates' ideas, handling classmates who shirk work, and expressing one's opinions—are highlighted and discussed by teachers.

With respect to will, research and theory suggest that students will develop positive emotional bonds to groups that meet their basic human needs for autonomy, belonging, and competence (Deci and Ryan, 1985; Connell and

Wellborn, 1991; Solomon and others, 1992). These positive emotional bonds in turn motivate students to maintain these groups and to internalize their values. The Japanese practices just discussed might meet children's needs and thereby promote their connections to school and internalization of its values in several ways. Japanese schools may meet children's need for *autonomy*—the need to shape the environment and to be free of arbitrary restraint—by giving all children a chance on a rotating basis to lead their classmates, by allowing children to help shape classroom rules and goals and to solve problems that arise, by emphasizing self-evaluation rather than evaluation by the teacher and self-management rather than adult control. Japanese teachers often use the terms *murinaku* (without force) and *shizen ni* (naturally) to describe children's natural acceptance of discipline that is not experienced as imposed from the outside.

*Belonging* is the need for stable, mutually satisfying relationships (Deci and Ryan, 1985). As noted earlier, Japanese schools emphasize belonging in several ways: by avoiding ability grouping and pull-out programs, by keeping teacher and students together for an extended period, by using special events to build a schoolwide sense of community, by emphasizing the importance of friendship and kindness, and by helping students develop connections to family-like small groups. The national course of study for elementary schools emphasizes goals—friendliness, persistence, cooperation, and energy—that all children can achieve, whatever their level of academic skills.

*Competence* (or *agency*) is the child's need to act upon the world successfully and to pursue activities regarded as worthwhile (Deci and Ryan, 1985). Children are likely to find school gripping and important to the extent that it connects with their natural quest to make sense of the world and to master it. In addition to children's active role in classroom management, several studies suggest that Japanese lessons are often driven by children's own thinking and may revolve around tasks that are inherently interesting to children, such as crafting boats that float, designing the ideal playground, finding out who works in each room of the school, and using measurement to compare objects around them (Stevenson and Stigler, 1992; Lewis, 1995). Such meaningful child-driven activities are much more likely to meet children's need for competence than is a focus on isolated skills whose purpose and meaning are not clear to children. Further, the weight given to goals such as friendliness, persistence, and responsibility also provides opportunities for all children to succeed at valued goals.

As we have seen, Japanese schools—like a number of U.S. schools—teach many component skills of conflict resolution, such as listening to classmates, explaining one's own needs, and intervening in fights. Japanese schools also emphasize the conditions—such as belonging, having a say in shaping rules, and making their own contributions—that are likely to bond children to school. Finally, they emphasize a particular set of values—friendship, cooperation, and solidarity—that provide a supportive context for conflict resolution and a spirit of self-critical reflection (*hansei*) that is likely to keep one practicing those values.

Cross-national research is best used, in Merry White's words, "as a mirror, not as a blueprint" (1987, p. 8). The myriad circumstances that vary across cultures make controlled comparisons impossible and imitation unwise. Yet together with U.S. basic research, Japanese practices suggest some interesting avenues of thought for U.S. educators.

First, can conflict resolution skills be built independently of other skills of self-management? For example, can children learn to take responsibility for solving conflicts at the same time that they learn to defer to adult directives in most other areas of classroom life, such as adult-imposed classroom rules and consequences? Or must the skills learned as part of conflict resolution—such as listening, asserting one's viewpoint, arriving at mutually acceptable solutions, and so on—be carried through many aspects of classroom life if they are to take hold? In Japanese classrooms, children's involvement in conflict resolution is part of a broad spectrum of responsibility for many aspects of classroom management.

Second, must conflict resolution skills be consistent with broader classroom values? Japanese classrooms emphasize goals of friendship, cooperation, and group progress, and students have regular opportunities to reflect on whether these values are being honored in their academic and nonacademic activities. Competition is generally avoided. In contrast, ability grouping, competition, and reward systems that promote comparisons among children tend to be much more common in American schools, leading to a strong (though perhaps not intentional) emphasis on being "the best." In contexts that generally emphasize winning over cooperation, conflict resolution may have little appeal to children—except in individual cases in which personal friendship or the desire to stay out of trouble motivates children to use these skills. Indeed, conflict resolution may be a form of losing the competition to be the best, rather than a means of achieving key shared values like friendship and cooperation.

Finally, we may wish to think of the will to resolve conflicts as a value that will be taken to heart by children if it is made explicit in the school setting and if students are predisposed—because of their positive emotional bonds to school—to internalize its values. If we follow this logic, then the school's success at meeting children's needs for autonomy, belonging, and competence, and thereby its success at promoting children's attachment to school, may become a critical determinant of the success of conflict resolution programs.

Comparative research on Japanese and U.S. schooling is in its infancy, and we cannot draw firm conclusions about differences in practice or in their effects. Yet both Japanese practice and U.S. basic research suggest that conflict resolution must be thought of as both skill and will. Conflict resolution strategies, it would seem, are unlikely to take root deeply unless students see them as valuable tools to be used in service of goals that they care about (such as cooperation and friendship) and to maintain the harmony of groups that they value (the class and school).

Whether students will be amenable to learning the skill and will of conflict resolution may depend, in large part, on whether schools meet children's needs for friendship, self-direction, and meaningful accomplishment. Japanese elementary schools—with their strong, nationally mandated emphasis on cooperation, friendship, children's contributions to group life, and classwide and schoolwide activities—have many qualities that help them effectively meet children's basic needs for autonomy, belonging, and competence. In return, children are likely to see school as a place responsive to their needs, and to take on willingly its values of cooperation, inclusion, self-discipline, and self-critical reflection. However, the specific values emphasized by Japanese schools may be somewhat different from those that Americans would choose to emphasize. For example, Japanese practices may emphasize harmony and sensitivity to others, while Americans would prefer a stronger emphasis on assertion and individual rights (Lewis, 1995).

At least one well-researched American program—the Child Development Project (CDP)—employs practices that are remarkably similar to Japanese practices, with the goal of creating a caring community for learners in order to promote children's social and ethical as well as intellectual development (Watson and others, 1989). More than a decade of longitudinal research comparing CDP schools and matched comparison schools indicates that the CDP program promotes both the skill and will of conflict resolution: it increases children's friendships, helpfulness toward one another, conflict resolution skills, commitment to democratic values, and experience of the school as a caring community. Although the CDP is based on Western basic research and theory about the conditions that facilitate children's prosocial development, its similarity to Japanese elementary practice is considerable (Lewis, 1995). It provides ample reason to believe that the strategies widely employed by Japanese elementary teachers—the emphasis on warm, stable personal relationships, opportunities for children to shape the environment, and highlighting of values such as helpfulness, kindness, and responsibility—may be important keys to the success of conflict resolution programs in the United States as well.

## Note

1. I am indebted to Marilyn Watson and her work on the Child Development Project for this idea.

## References

Connell, J. P., and Wellborn, J. G. "Competence, Autonomy, and Relatedness: A Motivational Analysis of Self-System Processes." In M. R. Gunnar and L. A. Sroufe (eds.), *The Minnesota Symposia on Child Development*. Vol. 23. Hillsdale, N.J.: Erlbaum, 1991.

Cummings, W. *Education and Equality in Japan*. Princeton, N.J.: Princeton University Press, 1980.

Deci, E. L., and Ryan, R. M. *Intrinsic Motivation and Self-Determination in Human Behavior*. New York: Plenum, 1985.

DeJong, W. "School-Based Violence Prevention: From the Peaceable School to the Peaceable Neighborhood." *Forum* (National Institute for Dispute Resolution newsletter), Spring 1994, no. 25, pp. 8–14.

Dewey, J., and Dewey, A. C. *Letters from China and Japan*. (E. Dewey, ed.) New York: Dutton, 1920.

Doi, T. *The Anatomy of Dependence*. Tokyo: Kodansha, 1973.

Easley, J., and Easley, E. "Kitamaeno School as an Environment in Which Children Study Mathematics Themselves." *Journal of Science Education in Japan*, 1983, 7, 39–48.

Kajita, M., Shiota, S., Ishida, H., and Sugie, S. "Sho-chugakko ni okeru shido no chosateki kenkyu" [Survey of teaching methods in elementary and junior high schools]. *Bulletin of the Faculty of Education, Nagoya University*, 1980, 27, 147–182.

Katz, L. "Dispositions as Educational Goals." *ERIC Digest*, 1993, EDP-PS-93-10.

Kotloff, L. J. "Fostering Cooperative Group Spirit and Individuality: Examples from a Japanese Preschool." *Young Children*, 1993, 48 (3), 17–23.

Kotloff, L. J. ". . . and Tomoko Wrote This Song for Us." In T. Rohlen and G. LeTendre (eds.), *Teaching and Learning in Japan*. New York: Cambridge University Press, 1995.

Lepper, M. "Social Control Processes, Attributions of Motivation, and the Internalization of Social Values." In E. T. Higgins, D. Ruble, and W. Hartup (eds.), *Social Cognition and Social Behavior: Developmental Perspectives*. San Francisco: Jossey-Bass, 1981.

Lewis, C. C. "Cooperation and Control in Japanese Nursery Schools." *Comparative Education Review*, 1984, 28, 69–84.

Lewis, C. C. "Japanese First-Grade Classrooms: Implications for U.S. Theory and Research." *Comparative Education Review*, 1988, 32 (2), 159–172.

Lewis, C. C. "From Indulgence to Internalization: Social Control in the Early School Years." *Journal of Japanese Studies*, 1989, 15, 139–157.

Lewis, C. C. *Educating Hearts and Minds: Reflections on Japanese Preschool and Elementary Education*. New York: Cambridge University Press, 1995.

Monbusho [Ministry of Education, Science, and Culture]. *Shogakko gakushu shido yoryo* [Course of study for elementary schools]. Tokyo: Gyosei, 1989a.

Monbusho [Ministry of Education, Science, and Culture]. *Yochien kyoiku yoryo* [Guidelines for preschool education]. Tokyo: Gyosei, 1989b.

Peak, L. *Learning to Go to School in Japan*. Berkeley: University of California Press, 1991.

Sato, N. *Ethnography of Japanese Elementary Schools: Quest for Equality*. Unpublished doctoral dissertation, Stanford University School of Education, 1991.

Shimahara, N., and Sakai, A. "Teacher Internship and the Culture of Teaching in Japan." *British Journal of Sociology of Education*, 1992, 13, 147–162.

Solomon, D., Watson, M., Battistich, V., Schaps, E., and Delucchi, K. "Creating a Caring Community: Educational Practices That Promote Children's Prosocial Development." In F. K. Oser, A. Dick, and J. L. Patry (eds.), *Effective and Responsible Teaching: The New Synthesis*. San Francisco: Jossey-Bass, 1992.

Stevenson, H. W., and Stigler, J. *The Learning Gap: Why Our Schools Are Failing and What We Can Learn from Japanese and Chinese Education*. New York: Summit Books, 1992.

Vogel, E. *Japan's New Middle Class*. Berkeley: University of California Press, 1963.

Watson, M., Solomon, D., Battistich, V., Schaps, E., and Solomon, J. "The Child Development Project: Combining Traditional and Developmental Approaches to Values Education." In L. Nucci (ed.), *Moral Development and Character Education: A Dialogue*. Berkeley, Calif.: McCutchan, 1989.

White, M. *The Japanese Educational Challenge*. New York: Free Press, 1987.

*CATHERINE C. LEWIS is director of formative research at the Developmental Studies Center, a nonprofit organization established in 1980 to conduct research and develop programs that promote children's intellectual, ethical, and social development.*

# INDEX

# ORDERING INFORMATION

NEW DIRECTIONS FOR CHILD DEVELOPMENT is a series of paperback books that presents the latest research findings on all aspects of children's psychological development, including their cognitive, social, moral, and emotional growth. Books in the series are published quarterly in Fall, Winter, Spring, and Summer and are available for purchase by subscription and individually.

SUBSCRIPTIONS cost $61.00 for individuals (a savings of 23 percent over single-copy prices) and $96.00 for institutions, agencies, and libraries. Standing orders are accepted. New York residents, add local sales tax for subscriptions. (For subscriptions outside the United States, add $7.00 for shipping via surface mail or $25.00 for air mail. Orders *must be prepaid* in U.S. dollars by check drawn on a U.S. bank or charged to VISA, MasterCard, or American Express.)

SINGLE COPIES cost $20.00 plus shipping (see below) when payment accompanies order. California, New Jersey, New York, and Washington, D.C., residents, please include appropriate sales tax. Canadian residents, add GST and any local taxes. Billed orders will be charged shipping and handling. No billed shipments to post office boxes. (Orders from outside the United States *must be prepaid* in U.S. dollars by check drawn on a U.S. bank or charged to VISA, MasterCard, or American Express.)

SHIPPING (SINGLE COPIES ONLY): one issue, add $5.00; two issues, add $6.00; three issues, add $7.00; four to five issues, add $8.00; six to seven issues, add $9.00; eight or more issues, add $12.00.

ALL PRICES are subject to change.

DISCOUNTS FOR QUANTITY ORDERS are available. Please write to the address below for information.

ALL ORDERS must include either the name of an individual or an official purchase order number. Please submit your order as follows:
    *Subscriptions:* specify series and year subscription is to begin
    *Single copies:* include individual title code (such as CD59)

MAIL ALL ORDERS TO:
    Jossey-Bass Publishers
    350 Sansome Street
    San Francisco, California 94104-1342

FOR SUBSCRIPTION SALES OUTSIDE OF THE UNITED STATES, contact any international subscription agency or Jossey-Bass directly.

# Resources *from Jossey-Bass Publishers*

## for Child Development Practitioners